Gretchen S. Bernabei | Jayne Hover | Cynthia Candler

CRUNCHTIME

LESSONS TO HELP STUDENTS BLOW THE ROOF OFF WRITING TESTS—

AND BECOME BETTER WRITERS IN THE PROCESS

Foreword by **Jeff Anderson**

HEINEMANN
Portsmouth, NH

Heinemann
361 Hanover Street
Portsmouth, NH 03801-3912
www.heinemann.com

Offices and agents throughout the world

The authors and publisher wish to thank those who have generously given permission to reprint borrowed material:

Portions from "Introducing Truisms with Picture Prompts" originally appeared in "The Insight Garden" from *Why We Must Run with Scissors: Voice Lesson in Persuasive Writing* by Barry Lane and Gretchen Bernabei. Copyright © 2001 by Barry Lane and Gretchen Bernabei. Published by Discover Writing Press. Reproduced by permission of the authors.

Portions from "Introduce the Concept" originally appeared in "Ba-Da-Bing! A Sentence-Imitating Exercise" from *Reviving the Essay* by Barry Lane and Gretchen Bernabei. Copyright © 2005 by Barry Lane and Gretchen Bernabei. Published by Discover Writing Press. Reproduced by permission of the authors.

Portions from "Minilessons" originally appeared in *Sparklers: High-Scoring Test Essays and What They Teach Us* by Gretchen Bernabei. Copyright © 2008 by Gretchen Bernabei. Published by the author. Reproduced by permission.

Library of Congress Cataloging-in-Publication Data
Bernabei, Gretchen S.
  Crunchtime : lessons to help students blow the roof off writing tests—and become better writers in the process / Gretchen S. Bernabei, Jayne Hover, and Cynthia Candler.
      p. cm.
  Includes bibliographical references.
  ISBN-13: 978-0-325-02673-2
  ISBN-10: 0-325-02673-4
  1. English language—Study and teaching (Elementary)—United States. 2. Language arts—United States—Evaluation. 3. Educational tests and measurements—United States. 4. Effective teaching—United States. I. Hover, Jayne. II. Candler, Cynthia. III. Title. IV. Title: Lessons to help students blow the roof off writing tests—and become better writers in the process.
  LB1576.B483 2009
  372.62'3—dc22   2009016227

Editor: Lisa Luedeke
Production: Lynne Costa
Cover and interior designs: Lisa Fowler
Typesetter: Gina Poirier
Manufacturing: Valerie Cooper

Printed in the United States of America on acid-free paper
13 12 11 10 09   ML   1 2 3 4 5

For Barry Lane

Who got us started on this path,

who sees and creates the best in people,

and who believes with faith in things unseen.

Ba-da-bing.

JAYNE, CYNTHIA, AND GRETCHEN

TEXT DUDE

there's a person at the center of all text.

CONTENTS

Foreword ix

Acknowledgments xiii

Introduction by Gretchen Bernabei xvii

    The Thermometer Rubric xvii

    Sharing Within the Profession xviii

    Two Teachers: Jayne Hover and Cynthia Candler xviii

    But Shouldn't Test Writing Be the Same as Real Writing? xix

    Knowing the Research xx

◼ Part 1: From Idea to Draft (Gretchen's Story)   1

Chapter 1 Selecting a Topic **7**

    Levels of Personal Experience 7

    The Quicklist 14

    Student Spotlight: Guadalupe 22

Chapter 2 Organizing and Prewriting Structures **24**

    The Talking List 24

    Writing a Kernel Essay with Text Structures 28

    The Flipbook 36

    The Fake Flipbook 54

    Student Spotlight: Esequiel 59

◼ Part 2: Revision and Development (Cynthia's Story)   61

Chapter 3 Writing with Style **65**

    Expanding a Sentence: Revision Stations 65

    Telling the Story, Asking Questions 73

    The F.I.T. Chart 77

    Sparkling Sentences 84

    Truisms with Picture Prompts 88

    Ba-da-bing Sentences 98

    Student Spotlight: William 102

Chapter 4 The Devil's in the Details **104**

    Great Beginnings 104

    Common Mistakes and Quick Fixes 109

    Preparing the Final Copy 112

Part 3: Crunchtime Tools and Minilessons

(Jayne's Story: Teaching Writing or Teaching Testing?)   115

Chapter 5 Countdown to the Test   **121**

    KISS (Keep It Surprisingly Simple): The Concept   121

    KISS Lesson Plans for Writing   123

Chapter 6 Minilessons with High-Scoring Student Papers   **130**

Appendix

    Research on Foundations of Effective Writing Instruction   137

    Beliefs and Experiences   139

    Student Chart for Brainstorming "Bank Experiences"   141

    Student Topic Lists   142

    Quicklists for Other Genres   144

    Connecting Life Experiences to Life Truths   146

    A Memory Chart   147

    The Story of My Thinking Chart   147

    Evolution of a Term Chart   147

    Discovering a Lie Chart   147

    Tribute to a Person Who Taught Me Something   148

    Backfire Chart   148

    Metamorphosis Chart   148

    Cause and Effect Chart   148

    Expository, I-Search, and Literary Analysis Text Structures   149

    Sample Pages of a Flipbook   150

    Revision Stations   151

    Cause and Effect (If…Then…)   152

    Student Self-Check Flipbook   153

    Student Self-Check Flipbook Final Copy   154

    Scoring Guide   155

    The Fake Flipbook   156

    Where's the BEEF?   158

    F.I.T. Chart   159

    KISS Lesson Plan   160

    Writer's Toolbox   161

    Minilessons   162

Works Cited   **165**

FOREWORD

You picked up this book to thumb through it for a reason. Perhaps it was the title or you knew one of the authors, but more than likely you picked it up, at least in part, looking for solutions, for ways to prepare your students for state and national writing performance tests. But I bet you wanted to find some lessons that will not only improve test scores but also prepare your students for all the writing they need to do for a life in the twenty-first century. Many would say the two are mutually exclusive. Not these authors. Let me tell you, finally a book like we all wanted has been written, and you have it in your hands.

First, you need to know about Gretchen Bernabei, a tireless supporter of students, teachers, and other writers. Much like the credit the authors give to Barry Lane—a man whose joy for writing and learning has influenced many of us— Gretchen Bernabei is quietly carrying on the work of her mentor, spreading accessible lessons and supporting teachers to share their successes on the page much like Barry did for her.

Gretchen Bernabei is a connector, and it's a good thing because she is connecting the readers of this book with two new voices of real classroom teachers who have scoured the face of the earth looking for solutions to writing tests that actually work—and who found a solution in Gretchen's writing and her workshops. But because of her humility, and her ability to connect people and ideas, Gretchen kept working with these two special teachers. Cynthia and Jayne took her ideas and played with them with kids, added to them, and altered them. Gretchen listened to them, cheering them on and visiting their classrooms. The result of all this interaction is *Crunchtime,* a culmination of conversations about what works. The result is a fine-tuned set of lessons that are good enough to be done throughout the year but are also quite helpful in—yes, I'll say it—preparing kids for a test.

Gretchen writes her mission is to "find, adapt, and develop lessons that are healthy for kids, that promote lifelong literacy" and these ways will just happen to "blow the roof off test scores." I'd add one more word to Gretchen's mission: joy.

She helps teachers and students find joy in writing again—or for the first time. She did it for Cynthia and Jayne, and now the three of them do it for us.

And the *Crunchtime* strategies do help improve students' writing performance for a reason. They are based in sound pedagogy and current research. Yes, test prep doesn't have to be worksheet after worksheet. In fact, you should know that this is not a series of practice tests or fill-in-the-blank worksheets, but rather lessons that excite and incite kids to write, to develop confidence, by actually doing the very thing they will be tested on—writing. It's common sense but not common practice. Gretchen, Cynthia, and Jayne make the journey toward better test scores simple and concrete, without insulting your intelligence or using one worksheet.

Just in the first few pages you will stumble into some gems that are so deceptively simple, it's hard to believe how effective they are. Gretchen, Cynthia, and Jayne give voice to what every good writing teacher has tried to say, but they do it with visuals and movement, which we know will help the ideas stick, and it's all done in seconds. I won't forget it and neither will you—or your kids. Check out the Text Dude.

But the list goes on. You will find ideas you may have used that worked a little, like keeping lists of things to write about, but Gretchen, Jayne, and Cynthia make the very concept simple and concrete—for the teacher and the student. And this bank of ideas, as Gretchen calls it, actually helps kids delineate what could become something of substance or worthy of their writing time—something many students struggle to get. With examples of ways to say things to your kids to get the ideas flowing, such as "list the memories you would choose to keep if a robot were erasing the rest of your memory tomorrow," you know you are in the hands of real teachers who work with real students.

If you have never experienced Gretchen's kernel essays, you are in for a treat. The same with Cynthia's flip book, or Jayne's F.I.T. lesson. These are all methods that help students begin to organize their writing. These strategies help students access the thinking they may not believe they have, but invariably that thinking will spew out when prompted with the lessons on these pages. Simple and concrete.

A trove of student examples helps each lesson become clearer, and some of the most delightful writing comes from their students. The truisms are my favorite. You might find yourself thinking, "Kids can do this?" Yes, they can, and together, these three master teachers show us how, step-by-step, inspiring hope in the hope-less, giving tips to the tipless, and filling those empty pages with thought and life.

Joy.

Yes, we can.

I think in these pages, Gretchen, Cynthia, and Jayne have lived up to their missions because each lesson fosters students' thinking and embraces their most human need for self-expression—and how writing is there for the taking.

—Jeff Anderson
Author of *Mechanically Inclined* and *Everyday Editing*

ACKNOWLEDGMENTS

From addressing envelopes to listening to my endless stories to being my greatest encourager, thank you, Jim, my husband, my best friend.

Gretchen Bernabei, thank you for birthing this dream and making sure it came to fruition. I absolutely love working with you.

Thank you, Judi Reimer, for the hours and hours of editing and preparation. You have such a gentle way of cracking the whip!

The story of the success from 69 percent to 97.5 percent would not have taken place without these incredible teachers and all their hard work: my dear friend, Carole Burlew; my first-year writing teacher partner, Candy Hines; Norma Sanchez; Cindy McCann; Linda Long; Patricia Quigley; and Phyllis Colbert. Thank you, Mr. Saucedo and Mrs. Fletcher, for having faith in us and letting us try. Thanks to Cindy Barnhart for believing in me as a teacher and for giving above and beyond as a principal. And thanks to my new principal, Mrs. Pollock, for her enthusiastic support.

And, finally, thank you to all my students for your willingness to give of yourselves. It is my privilege to watch you grow and to learn from you as you push me to be a better teacher every day. Marie, Brandon, Kiylei, William, Sallie—you inspire me, and Sallie, I am still waiting to stand in line to get your autograph on your own first book.

—JH

There are many who laid the bricks, one at a time, so that I could one day travel the road they built for me. I remember and remain thankful for:

My students—past and present, who have pushed, challenged, and inspired me to think harder and teach better. *As always: I love you. You are still the best.*

Dr. William H. Glaze, Dr. William B. Warde, and the late Mrs. Margaret Milke, who each, in their own unique manner as teachers, instilled a passion in me that led to teaching.

Beth Malone, who mentored my first year of teaching and taught me the importance of faith.

Glenna Edgin, whose willingness to go where I led and to lead when I faltered transformed our teacherhood into a sisterhood.

Kathy Horton, who has forever encouraged me with her belief that I could—as only a beloved sibling can.

Amanda Cox, a former student and friend, who gathered a troop of former students and made them all write to assure me that I was a good teacher and should write to publish.

Danielle Whiffen, who took a leap of faith as my principal and allowed me to teach by inspiration.

The many Terrell teachers who I have been privileged to work with through the years—teachers whose dedication and determination emboldened my own teaching, especially Virginia Fineout. *You're still my hero, Virginny.*

Erin, David, Katharine, Sean, and Sarah, my children, for all you've taught me along the way.

Judi Reimer, whose gifted revision has created and transformed in a most miraculous manner.

Gretchen Bernabei: *You graciously said you would; you faithfully did.*

Michael Melugin, my husband. Always.

—CC

For your encouragement and energy in the face of Texas two-steps, controlling oils, and deadlines, Lisa Luedeke, our Heinemann editor.

For freely comparing notes with me about more than teaching: gumball saint hunter Keith Perez, Jamaica truism queen Suzanne Deckert, the harmonious Eric Walker, football food translator Al Michalec, the photo-planting Gregory Reeves, linguist and veterinarian Stefan Tordai, and teaching colleagues Ginger Canaan, Latrice Caldwell, Katie Hodgdon, Mina Stecklein, Christine Ortmayer, Kristina McCalip, Blyth Swartsfager, Barbara Sullivan, Mia Rodriguez, and Condi Blair.

For working long and hard on behalf of children: Giacomo Leone, Marian McWhorter, Deb Stonich, Cynthia Holcomb, Kay Elaster, Maureen Ayer, Rebel Foster, Jenny Guerrero, Sondra Slivon, Elaine Weber, Robert Lewis, Roxanne Henkin, and the fellows of the San Antonio Writing Project.

For rocking my intellectual well-being, these pop star idols of the literacy world: Peter "resilience master builder" Johnston, Alfred "textual heritage man"

Tatum, Michael "no more assign-to-assess teaching" Smith, and the incomparable Thomas Newkirk.

For genuinely supporting this work, Dennis-Ann Strong, Larry Martin, Ken Patranella, and Dr. John Folks.

For helping me think and breathe, my longtime colleagues and friends, Patricia S. Gray, Dottie Hall, Alana Morris, Chris Goode, Cindy Tyroff, Suzi Lockamy, Kay Shurtleff, Sheila Hargett, Michele St. John, Becky Hoag, and Kimberly Grauer, and my sister, Sue King.

For writing and talking, pushing, waiting, putting up with me, and trying, my students at Holmes High School. I learn most from you.

For meeting me on Tuesday, my writing partner, Jeff Anderson.

For letting me keep coming back home and loving me wherever I am, Bert and Dixie, Johnny, Matilde, and Julian.

And thank you, Judi. Without your care, these lessons would be on napkins, coffee filters, and sticky pages, flying around Texas.

                                                              —GB

INTRODUCTION

by Gretchen Bernabei

The Thermometer Rubric

In the beginning, teachers wrote their own tests. I remember being a student, sitting in my chair at Horace Mann Junior High, breathing in the fresh, damp ditto fragrance from Mrs. Kramer's test. When I became a teacher, the vantage point changed—I got to carry the damply drooping purple pages over my arm and into my own classroom. I don't know what mimeograph machines or ditto pages cost, but it surely couldn't compare to what we spend now on high-stakes testing. Teaching has changed. More important, being a student has changed.

Starting around October of her third grade year, my daughter, Matilde, woke up every morning, padded into the bathroom, and slipped the thermometer into her mouth. She would concentrate and listen for the beep, hoping that she'd be too sick to go to school. It seems funny, but it's not. I understood. She had a life of drudgery: packets of work to be done in class; homework packets to work on before and after dinner; interminable, uncompletable packets, day in and day out. Children who didn't work their packets fast enough lost their recess and occasionally had to finish during detention. Matilde would look at me and whisper, "Please, Mom, don't write a note." Meanwhile, her school flew banners outside, proud of its exemplary status and its "Blue Ribbon" award—one of the nation's finest.

One day as Matilde took her temperature, I remembered my own third grade. It was fun. Donny and Ronny Barton were always funny, and Sharon Courville was my first best friend. Mrs. Cole was pretty beastly some days, but not every day; jump rope, freeze tag, and kickball reigned on the playground.

Something inside me hardened that year, watching Matilde with dismay. Our schools should be accountable, but do they have to become joyless halls of drudgery? I'm not against measuring student achievement and learning. But can't we develop lessons that use the best of what we know about learning and about children, lessons informed by research and results, lessons that include color, life, conversation, and laughter? That became my mission as an English teacher—to find, adapt, develop, and invent lessons that are healthy for kids, that promote lifelong literacy, and that almost coincidentally blow the roof right off test scores—and then to share these lessons with and learn from my teaching peers for the benefit of every Matilde in our data-driven land.

Sharing Within the Profession

Years ago, when my friend and mentor Barry Lane first told me that I should publish one of my lessons, I told him that I didn't have the first idea about how to publish something. He reached into his wallet and pulled out three phone numbers for me to call, numbers of people at three different publishing houses. "They'd want to see what you're doing," he told me. I was astounded. I had this image that people who write books would be competitive and guarded with information like that. As I wrote down the numbers, I said to him, "Barry, I can't believe you're helping me like this." He grinned and said, "Gretchen, we're all fighting the same battle. If we help each other, we all get stronger."

Since that time, I've shared with colleagues, through books and workshops, some ideas that work well in classes, especially with struggling students. In return, I've been gratified and exhilarated that many of them share back with me. While many teachers have contributed valuable thoughts and twists, two teachers in particular have knocked my socks clean off with their thoughtful inventions and triumphant successes in the face of harsh testing challenges.

Two Teachers: Jayne Hover and Cynthia Candler

Jayne Hover is a tour de force with her fourth-graders in San Antonio. She took an idea I shared with her about truisms and subsequently emailed me some student writing that was so insightful, so profound, and so abundant that I found myself scratching my head and picturing her class filled with child-sized Albert Schweitzers and Marie Curies. I was compelled to visit her class and watch how in the world she did it. Sure enough, her students weren't tiny Einsteins. They were real, shiny, squirmy children nestled into her classroom in this Title I school, jiggling and thrusting their hands up to read their writing, responding to the sounds of each other's voices and to her encouragement and leadership. I knew that not one of them would reach for a thermometer in the morning. And not only were her children enjoying their time in her class but their test scores caused a stir among area principals. Jayne's work over the next few years would continue to create such joy and consistently high scores that it was obvious we needed to clone her methods. She has taught me her ways, and I can vouch that they work with students well beyond the fourth grade level, even up to high school.

Cynthia Candler is an elegant seventh grade teacher in Terrell, Texas. When I met her, she told me in her hushed and velvet voice that although most of the students at her school were passing the state writing test, a high percentage of them were just barely passing. She was frustrated and desperate to improve their writing, to help them move toward "commended performance" scores. She herself had been a professional writer in her preteaching life, but she felt she needed to rethink what would help her students grow as writers. I shared with her what I knew about alternatives to the formulaic five-paragraph essay, and she went right to work with them. When I ran into her a year later, she showed me a glowing array of student work, using efficient twists I'd never imagined. I've been using and sharing Cynthia Candler's innovations ever since, and they have become a staple in many classrooms from elementary through high school. Oh, and test scores? Within two years, 42 percent of the seventh-graders at her school had "commended performance" on their writing scores.

But Shouldn't Test Writing Be the Same as Real Writing?

Is "test writing" a genre unto itself? Well, not exactly. Every state announces what kind of writing they'll test at what grade levels: persuasive, expository, literary analysis, personal narrative, descriptive, informative, combinations of these, or open choice. Each type of writing is authentically found in the real world, and it's reasonable to imagine that if we're teaching students to write authentically, then they will be equipped to score well on the tests. But it doesn't always work out that way.

Careful analysis of failing papers can reveal some of the differences between "real writing" and "test writing." For example, in the real world, a very brief persuasive letter to the editor might be powerful and accomplish its aim, but that same letter on a test could fail because it's not developed enough. It's not long enough. Or maybe the student didn't include enough ideas, even though the single point she made would have been effective in the real world. What makes a piece of writing successful? It depends on the situation.

So teachers must go beyond preparing students for successful lives in the literate world when we design our classroom lessons; if we don't, we may face chagrin when we receive our test results. We have to familiarize ourselves with what "the test" is really asking for and what the scoring rubrics really say. We have to become students of the details in the test. Is first-person writing acceptable? Are the students expected to repeat the prompt? Most states publish scoring guides that offer samples of student papers demonstrating the full range of scores, and these samples provide the best education for teachers interested in helping students.

Does this mean that students should write only practice test papers all year? Absolutely not. The best year would incorporate daily writing and reading activities, instruction that is fully informed by research about what helps students grow as writers, and instructional methods like those endorsed by the National Writing Project. Furthermore, one of our most important duties is to protect students from test anxieties. To that end, it's really most effective if students don't hear much about the test until the date is near. The teacher is the one who needs to be informed about the end result. So this book focuses on processes that will lead to a successful product. As stated by Lynnette Van Dyke of Michigan's Department of Education, "If you are interested in making real the central tenets of the National Writing Project, you have to attend to process as much as product. It seems as though we are focusing on product—people don't know how to get there." The lessons in this book are unified in their emphasis on process *toward* product.

Knowing the Research

The National Research Center on English Learning and Achievement published Judith Langer's *Guidelines for Teaching Middle and High School Students to Read and Write Well: Six Features of Effective Instruction,* which describes characteristics shared by the most effective schools in the study. The *Writing Next* report, published by the Alliance for Excellent Education, contains research findings outlining eleven elements found in effective writing instruction. Both of these reports echo the foundation beliefs of the NWP (see the Appendix, Research on Foundations of Effective Writing Instruction).

So what of research-informed classrooms? One would assume that students in classrooms incorporating these characteristics do well on tests, right? Well, they should—but they don't always. What happens these days when students fail a high-stakes test? At best, they shrug it off and do better next time. At worst, the student is retained at that grade, families feel pain, and schools are sanctioned or potentially shut down. Unfortunately, the problem often reflects students' inability to make connections between what they've been learning to do in class and how to apply it to a testing situation. For instance, how well are students likely to do on the district's "benchmark" test if they have been immersed in writing workshop or another form of process-based instruction? You guessed it—the scores predict poor performances.

It's crunch time.

We offer up the lessons in this book as strategies that incorporate the research, that engage students, and that can shore up some gaps between learning and testing. And one thing we know for sure is that when we use these lessons with our students, not one of them will say a silent prayer and reach for a thermometer.

From Idea to Draft

Gretchen's Story: Tracking the "Movement of the Mind"

S ometimes you can read one sentence and find yourself mulling that sentence over for years. One thought can spark a whole train of thought that lasts and lasts, like an Everlasting Gobstopper. I read a sentence like that recently; it was in Thomas Newkirk's monograph, "Reclaiming the Essay," from the Critical Thinking and Writing Series. He wrote, "If writing is to be a unique mode of thinking, we should ask how writing can foster and track movement of the mind." *That* was the sentence. I'd been thinking about how students respond to test prompts, wondering about how to move them away from the five-paragraph essays that they'd been conditioned to spit out in favor of something more readable, more inviting. And then that one sentence crossed my path. I've been chewing on it ever since.

I was teaching at Sandra Day O'Connor High School in San Antonio, and our state had just unveiled "the new test." We'd had such serious formula writing on our test for the previous thirteen years that I'm sure the people in our state department were impaling themselves on turrets near the state capitol. (Honestly, think about it. I get a little jumpy grading 150 essays at a whack. Can you imagine 150,000 essays? Wouldn't you grow just a tad murderous if you had to analyze very many of them?) At any rate, our state psychometricians unveiled for us the new test, with enough field-tested essays to demonstrate what they considered a failing 1, a barely passing 2, a higher passing 3, and the highest, a 4. We teachers leaned in to take a close look.

These new, improved essays were completely different—not only from the previous test's papers but also from each other. The rubric now asked for actual progression from one sentence to another and from one paragraph to another. In other words, the essay was expected to move from one thought to another, and the conclusion was expected to go somewhere new, not back to restate the introduction. In fact, the test authors used vehicle imagery to explain the evaluative thinking behind scores: "Here the paper spins its wheels until right here, where it engages and moves forward . . . and right here it stalls again; it goes completely off-track right here." Clearly, *wheels spinning* was repetition; *engaging* and *progressing* were points that evolved naturally one from the other; *stalling* implied vague or weird; going off-track needs no defining. In short, it sounded to me like our state was asking that the paper track movement of the mind! Well. About time.

My thought processes followed this train of thought: Do five-paragraph essays deliver what Newkirk described? Do they track movement of the mind? No, they don't. They don't show any movement at all. They tell what they're going to tell, then tell it, and then tell what they told. They don't go anywhere. This would explain why the general public doesn't enjoy reading them and why they exist only in schools. And this is why perfectly competent writing often doesn't score very high.

So I pictured the faces of students in grades four through twelve, frowning in bewilderment over this new direction. We'd have to figure out how to make this "movement of the mind" idea both simple and concrete enough that the students could follow some kind of structured steps, but flexible enough that it wouldn't become some new, dressed-up version of the five-paragraph essay.

I took another look at Newkirk's sentence. "If writing is to be a unique mode of thinking, we should ask how writing can foster and track movement of the mind."

What's in our minds? Thoughts, attitudes, beliefs, ideas, facts. How did those get there? That's the question, though it can take many forms:

What do you know, and how do you know it?

What's one thing you know, and how do you know that one thing?

What's one thing you believe, and what makes you believe it?

What's one thing you think is wrong, and what makes you think it's wrong?

What's something you know in your heart, and how do you know it in your heart?

What's something you know is true, and how do you know it's true?

What's one thing you think might be true, and what makes you think it might be true?

What's one thing you didn't always know but you know now? How do you know it now?

To make this concept come alive for students, I ask them to hold up their two hands, wiggle the fingers on their right hand, and repeat, "Everything I know. Every belief I have. Everything that's true. Everything that's not true. Every fact. Every opinion. Every thought for the day. Life lessons. Sayings. *Dichos.*" That's the right hand.

Then I have them wiggle the fingers on their left hand and repeat, "All my experience. Every place I've been. Every step I've taken. Everything I've seen. Everything I've eaten. Or smelled. Or heard. Every conversation. Every song, movie, book." That's the left hand. Once they have completed this short exercise, I show them the image in Figure A.

Figure A: Students let their two hands represent the beliefs and experiences they bring to their writing.

Check our website for reproducibles

Most really engaging pieces of writing have something from each hand.

Figure B: Notations on the hands prompt students to draw on their memories and beliefs.

Next, I ask the students to put their two hands together and ponder this thought: Every really good piece of writing has to have something from each hand. And the best ones weave the hands together. At this point, I show them the pair of hands in Figure B, pointing out the kinds of details they can draw on that are unique to them.

So which should come first in the composing process? It doesn't matter. Students could start with the left hand—their experiences—and then show their inner processing of that experience. Or they could start with the right hand—concepts, beliefs, or thoughts—and tell the story (or excerpts from their story) of how that thought has proven true in their lives. Either way, the resulting writing would be authentic, it would move, and it would be infinitely more readable than those school essays we've grown to dread.

And flexibility? Teachers could start with creating quicklists of memories, choose one and explore it, then deepen it with truisms. Or teachers could start with truisms and track the movement of the students' minds with kernel essays that have not just one set pattern but many possible structures. Then students could flesh out the kernel essays with some sentence expansion or Ba-da-bings or use a F.I.T. chart or whatever techniques teachers can cook up for their classroom menus. In any order, with any structure, if the student writers can clearly convey to another human being what they think and why they think it, then we have essays that would do well in life, as letters to the editor, as consumer letters to companies, as parent letters to schools, as interactions in their businesses, as family memoirs, as college essays, as academic writing, and most certainly as responses on writing tests.

We've put these ideas into practice in my school district, Northside ISD, and the results have been startling. Other teachers who have tried these ideas have seen results as well. Cynthia Candler, Jayne Hover, teachers throughout Texas, Michigan, West Virginia, Florida, California, New Jersey, Pennsylvania, Oklahoma, Georgia, and Minnesota have emailed to share their excitement and results. Our minds continue to move, and I have to grudgingly admit that facing the harsh reality of high-stakes testing has had some benefits, especially as we share with each other.

SELECTING A TOPIC

Levels of Personal Experience

THE PROBLEM: *The student's paper is boring because the topic is generic with details common to everyone.*

THE SOLUTION: *Using Levels of Personal Experience gives students a way to personalize general topics.*

"Using the 'bank' that's in my mind means not to write about something that's not important but to write about things that come from your heart. This helps my writing because it lets me know not to be afraid to write what I feel. It lets me know that I won't be judged for my truth."

—COLTON KUHN, SEVENTH GRADE STUDENT

■ HOW THIS LESSON CAME ABOUT

In spite of my best efforts to inspire them, my students' essays were full of identical, boring experiences. Their papers were trite and lackluster because their topic choices were filled with everyday experiences that were similar, if not identical, to all the other stories in the class. When a composition began, "It was Christmas morning . . . ," we already knew what happened before we heard the paper.

Then I discovered my "bank" analogy, and light bulbs seemed to go on.

"Each of us has a 'bank' in our minds where we 'deposit' the experiences in our lives that are too heavy to carry around with us every day," I told my students. "We own these experiences—they are a part of our lives and memories that will probably always be with us. But, like with 'big money,' it's not really safe to carry them around every day. If they were in the front of our mind, something might happen that we weren't ready to deal with around other people.

"So we bank them. We deposit them in an imaginary metal box, lock it, and trust that if we ever need them, they'll be there. But until then, they're safe in the bank and we can act like they don't exist. Doing this makes our lives easier.

"When you write, you need to 'withdraw' one of these experiences from your bank, because they are the real thing—not 'pocket change' memories. They made a lasting impression on you, and they will do the same for your reader."

As a group, we examined different topics and divided them into levels of experience. Level 1 memories were classified as "pocket change," and Levels 2–4 we called "bank" experiences. We decided that Level 4 memories would probably be too personal to write about, making Levels 2 and 3 the best choices for class compositions.

■ INTRODUCE THE CONCEPT

To show students how to pick a totally one-of-a-kind experience to write about, discuss the following levels with the class:

Level 1 experiences are:
1. everyday things that happen just about the same way to everybody.
2. the kind of thing you'd tell anybody about.
3. probably a lot more interesting to you than to anybody else.
4. boring to read because they are too predictable—we've been there/done that/know it already.

Level 2 experiences are:
1. more personal—although these things happen to other people, too, they happen differently for everyone.
2. the kind of thing you'd probably tell only your group of friends about.
3. interesting for other people to hear about—they want to find out what happened.
4. more interesting to read because they are not predictable.

Level 3 experiences are:

1. very personal.
2. the kind of thing you might write about in a journal or talk about only to your best friend.
3. something you normally tell someone only because you're unhappy and want some support.
4. extremely interesting to read because it takes courage and honesty to write them.

Level 4 experiences are:

…things that happen in your life that you probably never talk about, don't really want to think about, and will possibly never write a word about in your life.

Now challenge students to brainstorm a list of their personal experiences that fit Levels 2 and 3. Students will check with a partner to see if their topics are truly unique and then choose one to write about.

Debriefing

1. Did you choose an experience that you were a part of, that you saw with your own eyes and heard with your own ears?
2. Can you see this experience in your mind well enough to write about it? You won't need every little insignificant detail. You *will* want to examine the "frozen pictures" that you always see when you think about what happened.
3. Is this an experience where you might share some things you could have said/would have said/should have said but didn't at the time?
4. Can you match your "bank" experience to any of the prompts that you have seen this year?

Variations

1. Number a sheet of paper from 1 to 20. Challenge yourself to come up with as many experiences as you can think of in ten minutes.
2. Write the letters from A to Z down the side of a sheet of paper. Try to remember an experience for as many letters as you can.

When I challenged my students to illustrate their understanding of the Levels of Experience, one drew the hierarchy depicted in Figure 1.1.

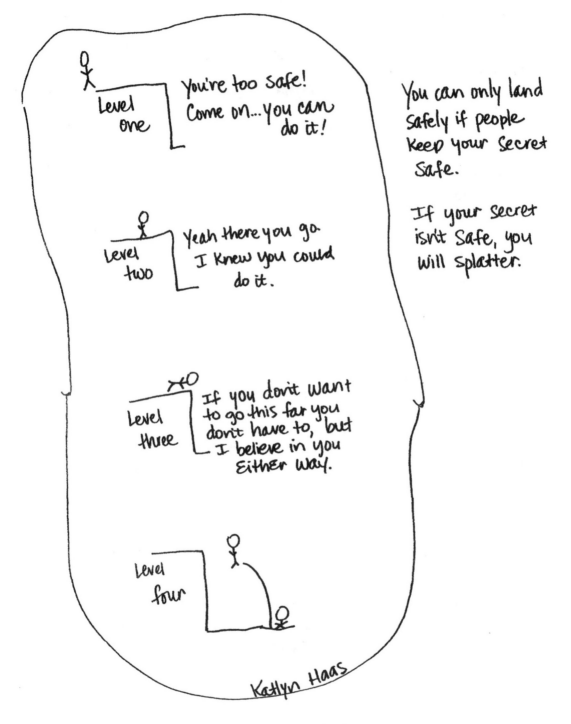

Figure 1.1: Student Depiction of the Levels of Experience

Teacher Reflections: Four Tangible Results

✓ *Students learned to distinguish superficial topics from more meaningful experiences to write about.*

✓ *Students using Level 2 and 3 experiences wrote with a much stronger voice.*

✓ *Finding one clear and important memory improved the organization and structure of student writing.*

✓ *Students were able to match their "bank" experiences to general interest prompts.*

■ EXAMPLES FROM THE CLASSROOM

Student Excerpts

Example of a Level 1 paper:

> "It was Christmas morning and we are about to open our presents . . . then we start opening our presents . . . it takes a long time . . . . Then we go to my mom's house . . . we eat and then we all start opening presents . . . etc."

Example of a paper written from a higher level:

> "As tears swam down my face, *Amazing Grace* was playing in my head. I watched in agony as my baby calf, Coffee, was lowered into the ground. My brother stood beside me with his hand on my shoulder telling me to be strong . . ."

Teacher Modeling Example of Making an Alphabet List

Suppose the prompt was to write about a time you had to meet a challenge.

B. Brother digging hole in yard for punishment and making me help
C. Cake I'd made falling on floor at my daughter's wedding
E. Erin calling from college crying her heart out
F. First day of teaching middle school
G. Getting to the hospital too late when my grandmother died

Someone who made a difference in your life	Something important you lost	A time that someone hurt you, or you hurt someone	Something unexpected that happened	An important memory	A favorite memory	Something you'll never forget

Figure 1.2: Student Chart for Brainstorming "Bank" Experiences

Check our website
for reproducibles

Student Chart for Brainstorming "Bank" Experiences

Figure 1.2 shows a chart we used to trigger memories that yielded plenty of Level 2 or 3 ideas. Once students filled in the chart, they always had a quick reference for starting a new piece of writing.

Examples of Levels

LEVEL 1 EXPERIENCES: Unless something *really unusual* happened with one of these experiences, you will not have an interesting story if you write about them. They may even have been fun, but they won't be fun to read. We all have these experiences, and we all know what happens.

- a birthday party (yours or somebody else's)
- what you got for your birthday
- what you got for Christmas
- getting your report card (good or bad)
- making a good/bad grade on a test
- getting mad at a friend
- breaking up with your boyfriend/girlfriend
- going to a sleepover
- learning how to ride a bike

- your baby sister/brother being born
- cooking dinner for your mother's birthday
- going over to a friend's house to play
- the game when your team lost/won
- going on vacation
- going to an amusement park or a water park
- the first day of school
- cheerleading tryouts (sorry, girls)
- football tryouts or practice (sorry, guys)

LEVEL 2 EXPERIENCES: These stories you would tell a group of friends.

- giving up on trying to learn something (piano, sport, and so on)
- someone at school wanting to fight with you
- helping a stranger
- friends talking behind your back
- brother/sister taking your stuff
- problem with a teacher or coach
- getting in trouble at home
- losing a treasured gift
- death of a pet

LEVEL 3 EXPERIENCES: These experiences you would share only with a trusted friend.

- brother or sister moving out of the house in anger
- being approached by someone to do drugs or alcohol
- taking something from a parent without permission
- death of a parent or sibling
- relationship problem with girlfriend/boyfriend
- parents fighting around you
- parent moving out or telling you they are getting divorced
- following along with a friend who is going to do something stupid or dangerous
- cheating in school

LEVEL 4 EXPERIENCES: These stories are too personal to write about for a school assignment.

The Quicklist

THE PROBLEM: *Students can feel trapped when they have a prompt and no ideas.*

THE SOLUTION: *Writing a quicklist is a painless way to give them choices of their own.*

"How can I write about an adventure I've had when I haven't had any yet?"

—VARIOUS STUDENTS

■ How This Lesson Came About

Every writing teacher has heard similar complaints: "I haven't got any memories like that." "I haven't got any memories at all yet."

It happens whenever students look at a prompt or a topic on the board. Some students will blurt out the complaint, but many more will silently think it. So one strategy for preventing the problem of the prompt versus the blank page is for students to create a list of memories to choose from. Any meaningful moments will do, and any meaningful moments in their lives will most likely connect to a surprising number of prompts from state tests.

Paula Brock, a wonderful teacher who wrote *Nudges: Thinking, Writing, Vocabulary, and Spelling,* suggests a listing activity for building topic banks for reluctant students. We've adapted her suggestion to include the kinds of memories that are often tapped as testing prompts.

■ Introduce the Concept

Begin with a class discussion. Say: "Let's talk about the difference between a moment and an era. How long does an era last? How long does a moment last?" (Discuss.)

"We're going to think of moments from your life that you might want to write about, so please take a sheet of paper and title it 'Quicklist!'"

Model on the board or overhead projector as students follow along on paper:

- Number your papers down the side, 1–12.
- For 1, 2, and 3, write down words or phrases that remind you of moments in your life when you were proud of someone.

- For 4, 5, and 6, write down moments in your life when you had to struggle in some way.
- For 7, 8, and 9, list the memories you would choose to keep if robots were erasing the rest of your memory tomorrow.
- For 10, write a memory involving an animal—someone's pet, a wild animal, or any animal memory.
- For 11, write a memory involving a gift you gave someone else.
- For 12, write down a time someone put money into your hands, any money—a nickel, a dollar, a check, any memory about money.

Now choose any three of these memories that you wouldn't mind letting other people hear about. Put a star by the one you'd choose to talk about first.

Debriefing

1. Of all the millions of moments you've experienced in your life, the one you put a star by bubbled up to the top. Why do you think that happened?
2. After any of these moments, were there some things in your life that you understood differently?
3. Can you connect any valuable life lessons with one of these memories?

Variations

1. Have students suggest additional categories for memories. (See Student Topic Lists, pp. 16–17.)
2. Take a collection of released test prompts from previous years and have students match them to topics on their quicklists.
3. It's easy to turn a memory into a piece of fiction. Students can pluck something from their quicklists and change whatever they want, creating fiction or outright fantasy.

Teacher Reflections: Four Tangible Results

✓ *Once students capture a memory on paper, they will never forget it.*

✓ *Frequently students share their writing with their family members, who voice how important those pieces of writing are to them as well.*

✓ *When students hear the memories of other students, their own lists grow. They are reminded of moments in their own lives that they had forgotten all about.*

✓ *After taking the test, students often remark that they wrote about a memory from their list, which made the blank paper that much less intimidating!*

Check our website
for reproducibles

■ STUDENT TOPIC LISTS

When asked to list things they could write a lot about, high school students suggested:

- the trauma of the emergency room
- the heartache of breaking up
- the fun of playing volleyball
- the heartbreak of losing someone
- the delay of the inevitable
- the joy of love
- the drama of friendship
- the instinct of survival
- the excitement of winning
- the fury of hatred
- the mystery of life
- the loneliness of being away
- the sadness of death
- the love of bubblegum
- the joy of writing
- the thrill of flying
- the confusion of life
- the horror of darkness
- the smell of an old book
- the excitement of new experiences

- the trauma of being lost
- the excitement of summer
- the sorrow of war
- the tragedy of time
- the shame of eating alone
- the stupidity of adults
- the fear of war in Iraq
- the melancholy of secrets
- flower pens
- bottle rockets
- Frisbees
- chocolate labs
- blue eyes
- license plates
- white t-shirts
- muddy tires
- braided bracelets
- ballpoint pens
- cowboy hats
- Superman
- planets
- red balloons

- diaries
- flip-flops
- lollipops
- crocodiles
- hospital beds
- money
- paint ball
- guitar strings
- rocking chairs
- tortillas
- church
- waffles
- beaches
- monkeys
- golf clubs
- hairspray
- tractors
- confetti
- diamonds
- sunshine
- wax
- pie

Fourth grade students suggested:

- horses
- monkeys
- dogs
- puppies
- flowers
- my own world
- my own horse
- fire
- vacations
- my teacher
- my friends

- my mom and dad
- my school
- someone special to me
- movies
- water
- my baby raccoon
- football
- basketball
- baseball
- the Army

- math
- NFL
- robots
- chickens
- United States
- national anthem
- money
- drawing
- history
- Indiana Jones
- school

- airplanes
- pizza
- my house
- ghosts
- a haunted house
- my cousin
- oceans
- lakes
- mountains

They also listed these "Stories I'd Like to Write":

- My Most Horrible Birthday (disasters)
- It Came from the Closet (scary)
- Frankenpizza (funny)
- A Diamond Robbery (mystery)
- A Fly's Life (nature)
- The Adventures of Bob (adventure)

▪ QUICKLISTS FOR OTHER GENRES

(Sample questions and sample responses)

Information Quicklist

Three things about the sky/planets/space you wish you knew:

1. How long will the sun burn?
2. Is there life out there?
3. Will we ever be space travelers?

Three things that are a danger to people:

1. Alcohol
2. Fast cars
3. Tornadoes

Three things that you wonder about bugs:

1. Do they have feelings?
2. Do they bond with their children?
3. Do they ever feel stressed out?

Three things that could make you sick:

1. Not wearing coats when it's cold
2. Being unfit
3. Not washing your hands

Three things that can make you healthier:

1. Exercise
2. Having friends
3. Eating right

Three things you know how to do:

Three things you know how to make:

Three things that have happened in your town in the past:

Persuasive Quicklist

Three customs/habits/rules at school you'd change:
1.   Get rid of school uniforms
2.   Make night school an option
3.   Let students request teacher/parent conferences

Three customs/habits/rules in the community you'd change:
1.   Enforce speed limits
2.   Add sidewalks
3.   Add a rec center in every neighborhood

Three customs/habits/rules in your country you'd change:
1.   Build bullet trains between cities
2.   Outlaw disposable food containers
3.   Lower the voting age

Three customs/habits/rules in your world you'd change:
1.   Get rid of light pollution
2.   Get rid of war
3.   End hunger

Three things you've bought in the last few months that gave you problems:
1.   Crest toothpaste—tube is hard to squeeze
2.   Black sweater—button came off
3.   DVD—skipped the first time we played it

Three people who should get awards for something:
1.   Giacomo Leone—most curious person
2.   Johnny Ponce—most patient person
3.   Dixie Shoopman—most wonderful mother

Literary Quicklist

A moment when a character changed:

1. The wolf's death
2. The first little pig's admiration for pig 3

A moment when a character tried to solve a problem:

1. When pig 3 took in pig 1 and pig 2

A moment when a character suffered:

1. Pig 2 during huffing and puffing
2. Wolf sliding into hot water

A moment when a character felt confused:

1. The moment the straw started to blow away
2. When the brick house didn't collapse

A moment when a character noticed a problem:

1. Pigs 1 and 2 when their houses started to collapse
2. When the wolf felt heat

A moment when a character tried to change something:

1. When pig 1 tried to talk pig 3 into building a faster house
2. When pig 3 tried to talk pig 1 into building a stronger house

Connecting Life Experiences to Life Truths

Students need time to reflect on their experiences to understand why the experiences stand out in their memories, what makes them important, and what they learned or how they changed as a result. The graphic organizer in Figure 1.3 gives students a way to sort through those experiences and understand their impact on themselves and others.

LIFE TRUTHS ▼

LIFE EXPERIENCES ▶

LIFE TRUTHS ▼	Family	Friends	Unexpected or Unusual	Sports/ Hobbies	Problems/ Change	Injury/Death	Traditions
It was hard to learn							
I had to make a difficult choice							
I made a serious mistake							
I wish I hadn't done it							
Someone had a positive influence on my life							
I had a positive influence on someone's life							
Life taught me a lesson							
It was important for me to accept responsibility							
I didn't see it coming							
It was important to me to be open to new ideas							
Where I was (my surroundings) affected my life							
It was important for me to accept someone for who they are							
I'm responsible for finding my own "happy ending"							
A favorite person/ place/time							
One experience can have the power to affect my life in a positive way							

Figure 1.3: Connecting Life Experiences to Life Truths

Check our website for reproducibles

■ EXAMPLE FROM THE CLASSROOM

Using the memory he listed as #7 from his quicklist, Julian wrote this two-minute quick write:

> We were at my grandfather's birthday party, and we were getting ready to leave. My grandfather was still in the kitchen, and he didn't know I was coming to say goodbye to him. I heard him telling my uncle something that I had said to him, and they laughed. My grandfather said, "That boy . . ." and the way he said it made me feel like they liked watching me, or liked how I'm growing up. I didn't know that he had actually been listening. I've learned that sometimes the one with the birthday is actually the one giving the best gifts.

In this case, Julian started with a memory, *what he experienced*, and added the life lesson, or *what he thought*. Julian did not sit down to write about "the best gifts," nor did the teacher ask him to write on that topic. The sense of play in this writing happens when a writer discovers "earned insights"—life lessons derived from experience. By adding more details, Julian could easily expand this into a full essay.

Student Spotlight: Guadalupe

When I visited Ed White Middle School last year, Rob Lewis and his students were deep in the throes of test preparations. He shared with me his students and their work. One of his seventh grade students was a quiet and beautiful girl named Guadalupe Moreno. She explained that one night, when she had been working on a writing assignment for Mr. Lewis's class, she had a dream about her sister's *quinceañera*, and that it was very fancy. When she woke up, she decided to write her dream. She wove into the piece the lyrics for "*Las Mañanitas*," a traditional morning birthday song. We read it together, and I was charmed. She had taken a Level 1 experience—a birthday party—and transformed it into something unique and memorable.

Check our website
for reproducibles

Las Mañanitas

by Guadalupe Moreno

On July 3 we had to get all the things for my sister's XV years party. She was so mad because she didn't have the chandeliers for her table. They had to go a little over budget. It was like she was a princess.

Estas son las mañanitas . . .

Then July 4 we needed to buy fireworks because we made a party in front of the church. It was just like my sister's XV party. There was a great mariachi playing on the church for the party. My dad had to order 300 fireworks.

Que cantaba el Rey David . . .

When it was July 23, my sister needed to hand out the invitation for the V.I.P.'s and the guests so she told me to help her. When we came back on her car, we invited the neighborhood. She wanted a big party with a lot of guests. That's what she got.

Hoy por ser dia de tu santo . . .

It was July 27. She was so happy to go and find a dress. She had something in mind. When she saw that purple, white, and light blue all together, she wanted that. When she went to fit it, she liked it. They needed to buy the white pair of shoes.

...te las cantamos a ti...

On August 1, it was my grandma's birthday. We went and surprised her with a cake. We invited her to eat and ate a piece of cake. We gave her our presents to her. One was the invitation and the other was a nice dress.

Despierta, mi bien, despierta . . .

August 26. It was so crazy. We woke up at 5:30 a.m. so we went to clean the front of the church. When the party started, it was so nice to see my sister on her dress, and her dancers were dressed so nice. The food was so good. There was rice, beans, meat, and mole.

Mira que ya amaneció . . .

There was a surprise. Me and my dad arranged this surprise. Her famous singer came out. She screamed. She was in the middle of the stage. The famous artist was Rakim and KenY, Los Super Reyes, and Los Kumbia All Stars. We didn't need to pay because the brother of KenY comes to the school that I go to.

Ya los pajarillos cantan . . .

We were dancing all night long with their songs. That was my sister Maria's XV party, and Ken Y's brother told me that he liked me and my sister's party.

La luna ya se metió.

A year later, I spoke with her again, and she recalled the dream, the piece of writing, and the subsequent test. "Did you write in a similar way on the test?" I asked her.

"No," she answered, explaining that she had written a more traditional paper for the test.

"Do you think that writing this piece helped you in any way?"

"Oh yes," she replied.

"How?"

"I knew I was going to do a better job."

Of course she passed. But more important, she had created for herself a whole new set of choices and experienced something wonderful while preparing.

ORGANIZING AND PREWRITING STRUCTURES

The Talking List

> **THE PROBLEM:** *The student says, "It makes sense to me," but the paper leaves the reader befuddled. The challenge for struggling writers is to find a topic and then stay with it.*
>
> **THE SOLUTION:** *Using a Talking List outline produces well-organized, focused papers.*

"Think what you need to say. Then say just what you mean. Make your words say just what you mean to say. Tell enough. Learn to say things in new ways. Listen for words that make you think of a picture. Tell the whole story. Leave out things that do not belong in the story."

—PAUL MCKEE AND M. LUCILE HARRISON, 1947

■ HOW THIS LESSON CAME ABOUT

Children need to think through their stories before they put them down on paper; otherwise, their thoughts are disorganized, unfocused, and confusing to most readers. For more reluctant writers or for writers who have difficulty organizing their thoughts, a talk-through can be a tremendous tool in their arsenal. Kids love this lesson because it does most of the work for them.

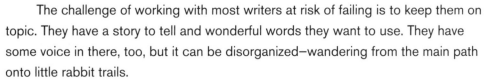

The challenge of working with most writers at risk of failing is to keep them on topic. They have a story to tell and wonderful words they want to use. They have some voice in there, too, but it can be disorganized—wandering from the main path onto little rabbit trails.

Webbing can be a helpful tool for prewriting, but we came to realize that it was confusing for those who struggled with organization. Our students wanted to write about each thing on their web independently, and it was difficult for them to focus on the main idea. Their composition ended up disconnected.

The Talking List works like an outline. It's a timeline of important events in chronological order that can be rearranged and edited for clarity. We have found that students who don't like to write rarely write in paragraphs. This exercise, adapted from Ruth Culham's *6+1 Traits of Writing* (Scholastic & NREL, p. 95), provides paragraphing painlessly.

▪ INTRODUCE THE CONCEPT

As with most new concepts, the most successful outcome begins with modeling the process. It's important for students to see that if all they have included are small details (labeled "Qs"), they haven't told us anything important. Conversely, if we have only main events, they've left out all the details. To help bring this concept home, try this method before the lesson: Prepare a transparency of a numbered list outline (in sequential order) derived from a favorite personal story or classroom experience. Leave out one important event and add an extraneous event. Model the process as follows:

- Tell your complete story to the class.
- Display the transparency. Have students identify the parts that they heard (label "✓" on overhead) and the parts not mentioned (label X). Add any parts students heard in the story that did not appear on the Talking List. Discuss.
- Label Talking List items *I* (for important information) and *Q* (for quick or small details).
- Look at each Q and decide which I it goes with. (This will create clumps.)
- Organize the list by rewriting the items labeled "I" in order and adding the "Qs" that go with it.
- Draw a line under each clump. (A "clump" is one "I" and any "Qs" that may be attached; these clumps will eventually become paragraphs.)

- Explain: "Remember when you first learned to color and people always told you to stay inside the lines? Remember how outlining your picture made everything look defined? The Talking List is an outline for your story to make your writing clear and easy to follow."

Practice Session

- Students will now make an outline list of their story (suggested time limit of three to eleven minutes). With a partner, students will exchange outlines and tell their stories. Their partner records a check (✓) by everything on the outline that the writer tells, marks an *X* on items not told, and jots notes for parts not in outline.

- With their partner's help, students label parts "I" and "Q," revise their own outline by pairing the "Is" with supporting "Qs," and draw lines between clumps for paragraphs. Students are now ready to write their stories. Remind students to stick to their Talking List; they can always add more details as they remember them when writing.

- Students will add an appropriate introduction and conclusion to their stories.

Debriefing

1. How did you feel when you could write just a word or a phrase?
2. How are you a better listener when you do this activity?
3. What did you like about this way of writing your story?

Variations

1. For younger or special needs students, write the outline for them as they tell their story. Go through each item and ask, "Do you think this was important in your story? Do we really need to know . . . ?" This will guide them as they make decisions about their story.
2. Have students record their story as they tell it to a buddy, and let them write their outline from the recording.

Teacher Reflections: Three Tangible Results

✓ *This lesson was the most effective one for raising the scores of struggling writers, because they now had a plan that told them where they were going and what ideas needed more attention.*

✓ *We noticed that students would immediately begin writing when they used the Talking List outline. Their story was before them, all laid out in paragraphs, but in list form. All they needed to do was put it together in sentence form.*

✓ *It was easier for my students to write on the day of the state test when they couldn't talk because they were used to thinking their story through. They had talked through their stories so many times before that on test day, they could talk inside their heads.*

■ STUDENT EXAMPLES FROM THE CLASSROOM

Fiona (Figure 2.1) and Brandon (Figure 2.2) used the Talking List to organize their thoughts and to select the elements they wanted to include in their story. Each produced a coherent and interesting story.

I	1.	When I was helping my dad
Q	2.	When he was painting
X	3.	~~When my mom told me to be careful~~
I	4.	When I hold the nail gun
I	5.	When I shot a nail
X	6.	~~When my mom got scared~~
Q	7.	My dad got scared
X	8.	~~Mom fainted~~
Q	9.	Went to hospital

Figure 2.1: Fiona's Outline and Subsequent Story

Gun Shot

As a little girl I helped my dad around the house. My dad is a carpenter. He painted the living room shiny red because that is my mom's favorite color.

My dad started to work on the crown molding. That is a piece of wood at the corners of the ceiling. I saw this tool and I was curious.

All of a sudden you hear a gun shot "Poow." There was only a single drop of blood on my shoulder. I did not cry but my dad was worried what had happened. I told him that my arm hurts. He tried to find more blood on my body but there was none.

My parents took me to the hospital. The doctor took out a one and one half inch nail from my shoulder. After that my parents don't let me be curious any more.

		Ever one has bad days
Q	1.	Stept in leftover pie
Q	2.	Mist the school bus
I	3.	Was in troble by parents for being late, got grounded
Q	4.	In class I asxedently bit my tongue
Q	5	Played basketball with Jonathan. We got mad.
I	6.	I lost my best friend

Figure 2.2: Brandon's Outline and Subsequent Story

Some People Have Bad Days

As I stepped out of bed my foot landed in some left over raseberry pie from last night! It felt mushy. Sense I had to wipe my foot off I mist the school bus. My parents were furios but they took me to school any way but I got grounded.

When I got to school I asxeditely bit my tongue by chewing on the inside of my check. Just a few minutes later after I bit my tongue school was over when I got home I played out side then my friend Jonathan came. We played basketball and I won. He said I let you win! I said yeah right so I walked of and while I was walking he pushed me so I pushed him back, and then we both went home and went our seprat ways. From that day on I learned that some people have bad days.

Writing a Kernel Essay with Text Structures

THE PROBLEM: *In between a prompt and a draft, students need structure and explicit, step-by-step guidance.*

THE SOLUTION: *Kernel essays provide an alternative to the five-paragraph essay, and every writer can do them.*

■ HOW THIS LESSON CAME ABOUT

Imagine your class. You say, "Okay, students, time to write a composition. Your job is to say one thing you know and tell how you know it. You have the rest of the class period. You may begin."

What would happen? Would the group nod, show outward signs of inner introspection, and quietly sit there producing said compositions?

A few might. Lysette would pleasantly blink a couple of times and start writing. But Eduardo would want to know exactly how to tell "how you know it." Ashley would ask, "One thing we know about what?" Jesse would ask for an explanation from the beginning again. Jonathan would put his head down until the bell.

Students need guidance, and a kernel essay is an ideal scaffold to help them get started. It provides students with a concrete strategy for translating thought into sentences that will eventually result in a paragraph, or an essay, or any other form of writing that serves their purpose—one sentence for each step of the thought process. The following introductory lesson is the simplest way to ease students into the kernel essay process, beginning with a narrative of a personal moment and a text structure called "A Memory."

■ INTRODUCE THE CONCEPT

Hold up an imaginary kernel of corn and ask, "What could you do with a kernel of corn?"

"Eat it!"

"Plant it and grow a whole plant."

"A whole cornfield!"

Which answer is correct? It depends on what you want. They're all correct. The same is true of a kernel essay. You could expand it into a full novel or a movie script. Or it could certainly be expanded into a two-page composition (see "Expanding a Sentence," p. 65). Often, it's perfect just as it is, suitable for formatting and framing as a gift, with or without added photo graphics. Tiny but packed.

Whole Class

- Put the memory text structure (Figure 2.3) on an overhead projector, covered up.
- Ask students to select a moment from a Quicklist (see "The Quicklist," p. 14).
- Give students these directions: "Number your papers one through five. Think about the moment you chose. I'm going to ask you five questions about that moment, one at a time. Answer each question about that moment."
- Then ask the following questions:
    1. Where were you and what were you doing?
       (As the students write, uncover the first box on the overhead.)
    2. What was the first thing that happened?
       (As students write, uncover the second box on the overhead.)
    3. What was the second thing that happened?
       (As students write, uncover the third box on the overhead.)
    4. What was the last thing that happened?
       (As students write, uncover the fourth box on the overhead.)
    5. What did you think about just then?
       (As students write, uncover the last box on the overhead.)
- Now ask them to remove the numbers.
- Explain that they now have written a kernel essay. It's like a kernel of corn, tiny but packed.
- Let them read their kernel essays to a partner or group just to see what they said.
- Repeat this process on two or three subsequent days, and let students choose a kernel essay to expand.

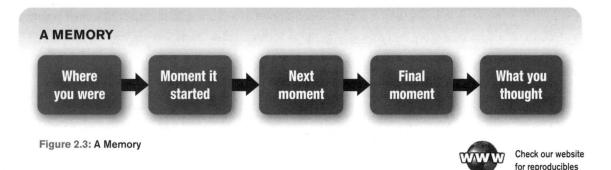

A MEMORY

Where you were → Moment it started → Next moment → Final moment → What you thought

Figure 2.3: **A Memory**

WWW Check our website for reproducibles

This exercise works very well with narrative text structures. Try some variations (Figures 2.4–2.7) as students become familiar with the process. But what about academic writing? Or expository writing? Could the text structure format for narrative writing be useful to students asked to write a summary of a science experiment or a literary analysis? Consider your own thoughts. Each one has a history, a life story. Each began somewhere, had an infancy as an inkling, grew toward a question or a notion, either fell off or continued to grow into a mature concept, accepted fact, or real belief. You could even create a timeline for the life of any thought, idea, or belief that you contain.

So text structures work for expository and literary prompts as well as narrative. It seems that the more of our personal discovery process we put into the information, the more readable it will be to someone else. Looking into sources like *The Best American Science Writing* (from the Best American Series), you will find that these text structures incorporate authentic research and expository information into similar thought-tracking structures. And if you add an audience and an agenda, these also serve as persuasive structures.

Debriefing

1. Was this easy?
2. Why did it work/not work?
3. Do you realize that you have a beginning, a middle, and an end?
4. Did anyone feel "oh no!" when I got to number four and asked you to write the last thing that happened? Did you need to put in another thing that happened? Or two more? (When this happens, draw a new text structure, with boxes as the student needs them.)
5. Introduce variations. Name finished text structures after the students who completed them and leave them up. Soon there will be variations all over, and other students will begin to invent their own structures.

Variations

A kernel essay is simply a sentence-by-sentence summary of the main points of a story that makes an outline for the writer. With text structures, students write one sentence for each box.

A Memory: The basic form, as we saw in Figure 2.3, might result in this story:

- We were gathered at the windows watching the rain.
- My Aunt Sue was getting dressed.
- The phone rang, and we heard that the preacher was lost.

- Several hours later, the wedding happened.
- Rain and traffic can't spoil a good romance.

The Story of My Thinking (Figure 2.4): This twist encourages students to document a change of opinion:

- I used to think that you had to be a special personality type, like a pirate or a trick rider, to have adventures.
- But then our family spent some time on my grandfather's farm.
- And now I think that real adventure can be in all kinds of backyards, ready for everyone.

Check our website
for reproducibles

TRUISM: *You can find adventures anywhere in life.*

THE STORY OF MY THINKING

| What I used to think | ➡ | but this happened | ➡ | so now I think |

Figure 2.4: The Story of My Thinking

Evolution of a Term (Figure 2.5): Here, students can see how their thinking changes over time:

- When I was four, adventure was a herd of tricycles in the driveway.
- When I was ten, adventure sounded like hoof beats on my grandfather's farm.
- Now, adventure means being an activist for a better world.
- When I'm old, adventure will be vicarious: The thrill will be in hearing about my children's adventures.

Check our website
for reproducibles

EVOLUTION OF A TERM (WORD OR PHRASE IN THE PROMPT)

| What the word meant to me when I was four | What the word meant to me when I was eight | What the word means to me now | What the word will probably mean when I am _____ (pick an age) |

Figure 2.5: The Evolution of a Term

Discovering a Lie (Figure 2.6): Students think back on an old belief and relate how they learned the truth. Many will probably reflect on how they felt about the revelation:

Check our website
for reproducibles

- When I was little, my parents told me about the Easter bunny.
- So I believed that every Easter he came along and hid eggs and presents for me.
- Then one year I saw my father hiding the eggs.
- Now I realize that my parents wanted me to have a good childhood.

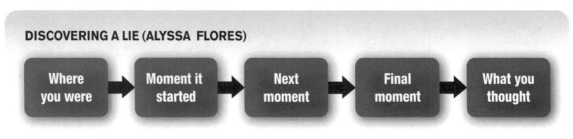

DISCOVERING A LIE (ALYSSA FLORES)

Where you were → Moment it started → Next moment → Final moment → What you thought

Figure 2.6: Discovering a Lie

The variations are as diverse as your students. See Figure 2.7 for four more text structures students may wish to use, or invite them to create their own.

Kernel Essay Text Structures for Other Genres

As we have discussed, other genres are equally accessible through this activity. See Figure 2.8 for text structures that work with expository writing, an I-search paper, or literary analysis.

Teacher Reflections: Four Tangible Results

✓ *You see students' need for a firm grip on a definite structure, like holding onto a steering wheel tightly. As they become comfortable with the structure and the kernel essay process, they begin to feel comfortable changing the structure. Before your eyes, they can develop fluency with creating their own structures, and your wall fills up with structures they have invented. They still need a steering wheel, but they like being in charge of where the car goes.*

✓ *On test day, students often squander their own stamina by writing lengthy first drafts on the practice paper. Writing kernel essays is both time-saving and strength-preserving for our young writers.*

✓ *Students voice appreciation for so much result with so little drudgery. "I can know in four short sentences if I have something worth working on," Heather told me.*

✓ *Students who know how to use kernel essays and text structures now have an alternative to the standard five-paragraph essay.*

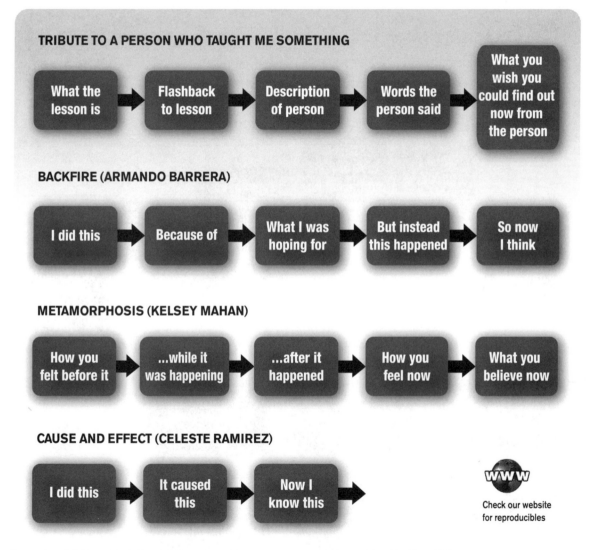

Figure 2.7: Additional Variations—Tribute to a Person Who Taught Me Something; Backfire; Metamorphosis; Cause and Effect

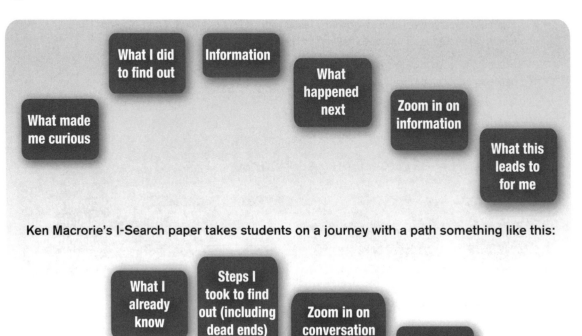

Ken Macrorie's I-Search paper takes students on a journey with a path something like this:

How One Event Changed a Character, and Here is How You Could Tweak It Further for Literary Analysis

How a character was before	What happened	How the character changed

Or...The Story of a Character's Thinking

What the character used to think	What happened	What the character thinks now

Check our website
for reproducibles

Figure 2.8: Expository, I-Search, and Literary Analysis Text Structures

■ STUDENT EXAMPLES FROM THE CLASSROOM

A Memory

I was in the hospital waiting room with my dad while my mom was having a baby.

A lady came to get us.

We went into Mom's hospital room.

I saw my baby brother for the first time.

Life is a miracle.

The waiting room at the hospital smelled like disinfectant and medicine. All of the couches and chairs were full with people reading, sleeping, staring off into space—all waiting for someone to walk in and tell them that the family's new baby had been born.

We were waiting, too. My dad was trying to read a magazine. I noticed that he was having trouble focusing. I guess it's hard to read something when your eyes keep wandering to the door.

I wasn't doing any better. Even though I was sleepy, my eyes wouldn't stay shut. I kept looking at the door, too, wondering how my mother was doing and when my brother would finally get here. I wasn't really nervous . . . or was I? Surely everything would be OK with my mom . . . or would it?

In the middle of my confused thoughts, a lady in a green suit walked through the waiting room door and asked, "Is there a member of the Smith family here?" After sitting for so long, my dad nearly fell over when he jumped up to answer her. I couldn't move, suddenly afraid that one of a million things might have gone wrong.

Somehow, though, putting one eager foot in front of the other, we found ourselves at the door to her room. We saw my mom staring into the wadded blanket in her arms. Then the blanket cried. The sound made me want to cry, too, but I was afraid my mom would think I was jealous or disappointed. She looked at us, smiled a huge, tired smile, and held the blanket up for us to see. We all saw my brother for the first time, all red-faced and sleepy. And beautiful. Wow! I thought. I just met him so how can I already love him so much? The words "I'm a big sister now" kept getting louder and louder in my head, until I thought my brain would explode.

Life is a beautiful miracle. And our little miracle was staring right at *me*.

The Flipbook

THE PROBLEM: *All the students say, "I need your help!" every step of the way.*

THE SOLUTION: *Using the flipbook, which gives students a clear and creative resource for organizing and completing a writing piece more independently.*

"I don't have to 'teach for the test' anymore. I teach real writing."

–CYNTHIA CANDLER

■ HOW THIS LESSON CAME ABOUT

The scene in many classrooms in the weeks before the standardized test looks something like this: "Miss _____, will you read this?" The teacher looks at this student's writing, nervously aware that there are four other hands in the air and the period is half over. "I'll be right with you. Hold on." Their hands drop, and they sit, patiently doing nothing. Two or three minutes go by, and the teacher moves to the next student. "Am I doing this right? Is it *good*?" This moment is critical in a writing classroom, because it is the moment that a potential *transfer of responsibility* hangs in the balance between student and teacher. The writer translates "yes" to mean that everything he's written is perfect and proceeds accordingly. "No" brings on the inevitable questions, time-consuming and constraining in a large class. There's just not enough time.

Many students try to write a composition without a prewriting activity that allows both the student and the teacher to examine where that writer will be going and to determine, before the entire composition is committed to paper, whether the direction of the writing is likely to be successful.

I found there were never enough classroom minutes for me (Cynthia) to encourage, guide, or redirect each student who needed my input, and every period became a frustrating race against the clock. That's when I began to use the flipbook, a set of folded, stapled papers that make a booklet for organizing and expanding a student's writing.

Combined with Gretchen's kernel essay, the flipbook provides a workable organizational strategy without relying on the five-paragraph essay format. It brings concrete order to a complex skill: For the student, the flipbook acts as a sequenced, step-by-step guide for writing; for the teacher, the lessons demonstrating good writing techniques can be matched to the student work in progress. By providing a designated amount of space that requires a designated amount of writing about *one* event in the writer's story, a potentially intimidating assignment becomes a manageable and logical process.

The flipbook also allows students the flexibility to move around in their piece, working on different sections while they wait for the teacher to answer whatever questions come up. Their writing becomes more independent, more confident, and more creative. They look forward to working on their essays, and they don't waste precious classroom minutes sitting with their hands raised waiting for the teacher. This strategy supported our efforts toward the elusive goal of teaching *real* writing within an authentic classroom writing experience.

■ INTRODUCE THE CONCEPT

Before the lesson: Have the students Select a Topic (see p. 16) and write a Kernel Essay (see p. 28). Discuss the importance of having a specific reader in mind. Make flipbooks for each student (see "Step-by-Step Directions," p. 43) and a large sample or overhead transparency for modeling as the students fill in their booklets.

Step 1: Filling in the Flipbook

Flipbooks can be used for almost any written format. When I first introduce the concept, I often start with a letter—in this case, a letter to someone who shared a moment that changed your life or taught you something important.

Show students a completed flipbook and read through it with them. Describe the terminology (see Figure 2.9a), and then take them through the process step-by-step.

- Each folded-down section on the front is called a "flip." Have students write their topic on the cover (see Figure 2.9 b).
- Turn the flipbook over to the back side. Have students write the questions from their kernel essay on the back with a brief answer for each question (see Figure 2.9c).

Kernel Essay Questions
1. Where am I? What am I doing?
2. What happened first?
3. What happened next?

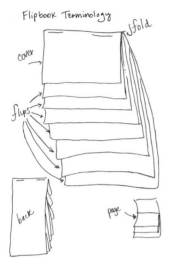

Flipbook Terminology

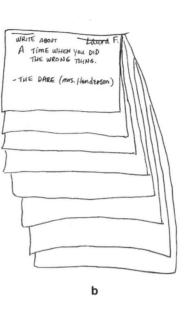

b

c

Figures 2.9a–2.9e:
Sample Pages of a Flipbook

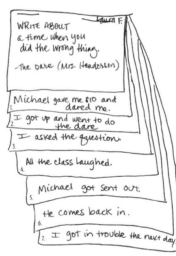

d

e

4. Next?

5. Next?

6. What happened last?

7. Final thoughts.

Turn the flipbook back over to the front. Copy the *answers* to each question from the back of the flipbook on to each of the numbered "flips" (see Figure 2.9d).

Step 2: Expanding the Kernel Essay Sentences with Revision Stations

- Have students fold up the cover and look at the sentence showing on Flip 1. They will write all the details about this event on the inside page (see Figure 2.9e). They can write on the back of the flip if needed, but they are *not* allowed to add any information or move on to the next event (which is on Flip 2).

- Introduce and discuss Revision Stations (see Figure 2.10) and how to use guiding questions. Students can rotate through the stations as they fill in the inside pages of their flipbooks.

Check our website for reproducibles

REVISION STATION 1: SNAPSHOT CHALLENGE

1. Look at your sentence.
2. Imagine that you're looking at a photograph (or snapshot) taken at that moment.
3. Use words to describe everything you can see in the snapshot.

REVISION STATION 2: SENSES CHALLENGE

1. Look at your sentence.
2. Write details to show every one of the senses:
   → What did you see?   → What did you feel?
   → What did you hear?   → What did you taste?
   → What did you smell?

REVISION STATION 3: THOUGHTSHOT CHALLENGE

1. Look at your sentence.
2. Imagine that people could hear everything you were thinking at that moment.
3. Write down everything that went through your head, everything you thought right then.

REVISION STATION 4: DIALOGUE CHALLENGE

1. Look at your sentence.
2. Imagine all of the conversation that went on at that moment.
3. Write down everything everyone said.

REVISION STATION 5: BA-DA-BING CHALLENGE

1. Look at your sentence.
2. Write one Ba-da-bing sentence for that moment, with these three parts:

Where your feet were right then

What your eye saw right then

What you thought right then

Figure 2.10: Revision Stations

- Continue turning up each flip and filling in the important information for each one. This will take several days to do well. Use Flipbook Minilessons on Great Beginnings (p. 104), Common Mistakes (p. 109), and The Final Copy (p. 112) as needed.
- When students have finished the flipbook, they are ready to transfer their story to paper.

The Payoff

The results of this strategy are amazing. In addition to the advantages already mentioned, there are some added benefits. For instance, when students are stuck on a particular section, the empty space on that page opens a door for targeted minilessons for their writing. A second bonus is the great head start it gives the writer: When the flipbooks are completed, students can already see an almost finished composition, ready to be transferred to paper. Nearly all the responsibility has been neatly shifted from teacher to student, from instructor to writer.

In our school, scores had already been fairly strong, especially for a Title I school, but as the test scores came back after using the flipbook, the results spoke for themselves. Passing scores climbed from 91 percent to 98 percent, which was a thrill, but we were equally surprised by the solid increases at the higher levels. The year before, 91 percent of our students passed with a composition score of 2 or better, but only 36 percent reached the state Commended rating. The year we introduced the flipbook, 42 percent of our students achieved Commended, papers scoring a 3 jumped from 128 to 147, and papers scoring 4 went from 12 to 18 (see Figure 2.11).

QUICK TIP: The state writing test doesn't allow the use of flipbooks, so my students ingeniously devised a fake flipbook strategy (see p. 56).

Year	% Passing	% Commended	Score 1	Score 2	Score 3	Score 4
2005	91%	30%	17	130	92	6
2006	91%	36%	9	129	128	12
2007	98%	42%	7	87	147	18

Figure 2.11: **Comparison of Scores Before and After Flipbook**

Debriefing:

1. How did using the flipbook help you match an experience to the prompt?

2. How did thinking about the real person you were writing to improve your paper?

3. Why did this seem more like real writing and not just a school assignment?

Variations:

1. The cover can be divided into boxes for clarification (see Figure 2.12).

2. Paragraphing can be easily and naturally taught using each event (that is, one page of the flipbook) as a reminder to start a new paragraph.

3. See Dinah Zike's *Big Books* and *Notebook Foldables*® for other ideas for paper booklets.

Teacher Reflections: Four Tangible Results

✓ *Students work more independently and confidently with less teacher input while using the flipbook.*

✓ *Craft lessons can be designed to meet specific student needs.*

✓ *Students can move around in their writing piece, choosing when and where to work on a section.*

✓ *The kernel essay combined with the flipbook provides both teacher and student a quick and easy way to examine the sequenced structure of the writing before transferring it to paper.*

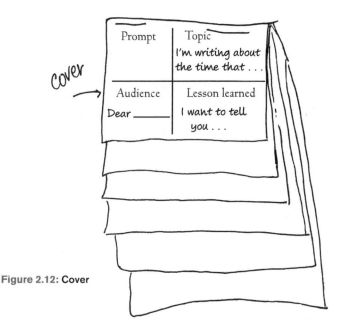

Figure 2.12: Cover

■ EXAMPLES FROM THE CLASSROOM

An example of the results of the flipbook process follows. Consider the kernel essay and full essay of seventh grader Laura Flores:

Kernel Essay

I was in AIM Reading class.

Michael gave me $10 and dared me.

I got up and went to do the dare.

I asked the question.

All the class laughed.

Michael got sent out.

He comes back in.

I got in trouble next day.

Full essay

I was in AIM Reading class last year, copying notes from the board, not knowing all the excitement that was about to begin. Michael was the new kid in the class. He had just moved from regular reading to Aim Reading. Anyway, we were sitting there, copying the notes and all of a sudden he says, "I'll pay you 10 bucks if you go up to Ms. Henderson and ask her if her chest is real."

"Yeah right," I said, "I bet you don't even have the money!" He signaled me to look down and took out a crumpled 10 dollar bill. Oh my God, I said to myself, should I? Well, it is just a joke and I guess I won't get in trouble so . . .

Without thinking about it again I said, "Okay." He gave me the money and I got up and walked to Ms. Henderson. I didn't feel like myself, I felt like someone else was inside me, taking over my body. I looked at Michael, who was looking at me daringly. I can do this! I said to myself. I'll give everyone a big laugh, go home and spend my profit. What a nice guy! We'll have a big laugh after this funny joke.

After what seemed like hours of walking, I got in front of Ms. Henderson. I started to regret it, but my body was out of my control.

"Ms. Henderson," I started, "somebody told me to ask you this . . ." I kept stopping as she turned around looking serious. I'll get her in a good mood. I said to myself. I resumed, "Somebody told me to if . . . uh . . ." The room suddenly grew quiet, as if wanting to hear what I was going to say.

"Okay, somebody wants to know if your, uh . . . if your chest is real."

The silent room suddenly burst in laughter from all the kids in the room. The loudest laugh was Michael. I looked around the room. Everyone's faces looked like red tomatoes. The class sounded like wolves, with all the howling of laughter. Some people were even choking!

"Be quiet!" Ms. Henderson exploded with embarrassment. I was expecting her to be laughing with the rest of the class. Everybody got quiet, except for Michael, who was howling with laughter.

"Get out!" she screamed furiously at Michael. He obediently got quiet, got up and left the room.

"Go sit down." She said patiently to me. Oh shoot, I thought, now me and Michael are in trouble!

After 10 minutes or so, he came back in. "You're a daredevil!" he told me. "I never thought you were actually gonna do it!" I couldn't help it, but to smile a little. I felt happy. I knew I wouldn't be alone on my punishment. I wasn't thinking when I dug my hand into my pocket and took out the 10 dollar bill he had given to me, and I gave it back to him. He looked so scared, I felt bad for him.

Ms. Henderson reported us to the office, and the next day, both of us went to I.S.S. I had three days, and he had five. It was really fun though. The teacher there was really nice. It was better than a regular class, better than my most favorite class. I enjoyed it a lot, but I'm better off with a good reputation.

Bad things don't come by themselves, but because someone brings them.

▪ STEP-BY-STEP DIRECTIONS FOR MAKING A FLIPBOOK

Flipbooks can be made in any size and with different numbers of pages, depending on the needs of the students and the assignment. One possible format follows:

- Get lots of assorted color construction paper, 9" x 12". (Take out the blue and the black, because they are too dark to write on or to read from.)
- Four sheets of construction paper will make two flipbooks, so divide paper into stacks of four sheets each.
- Portrait-fold a stack of four sheets in half, mark the top and bottom with a dot, and cut all four sheets at once with a paper cutter.
- Take one set of papers and pull the top three sheets downward so that four evenly spaced flips are created.

- Fold all four sheets forward to form a booklet, crease, and staple at the top (See Figure 2.13).
- Use the structure in Figure 2.14 to set up your flipbook.

QUICK TIP: I use a production-line technique when making flipbooks: Separate paper, stack in fours, cut all the stacks, shift and fold, then staple. It goes much faster if you don't pick up–and put down–the stapler several hundred times.

Because the flipbook lesson will take several days, additional Debriefing Questions, FAQs, and a Cause and Effect chart to be used during the unit follow:

Debriefing Questions for Flipbooks

1. Tell me three problems you had with filling out the flips and/or the pages.
2. Were your kernel-essay sentences *actions* (things that *happened*) or were they thoughts or feelings?
3. If they were actions, did you have enough pages to easily divide up the story?
4. Did anyone use fewer than seven flips? How did that work out?
5. Did anyone wish they had another flip? If so, how did you handle that? Did it work? Were you satisfied with how it turned out?
6. Ask three questions, now that you've done it once, about how to fill out the pages.

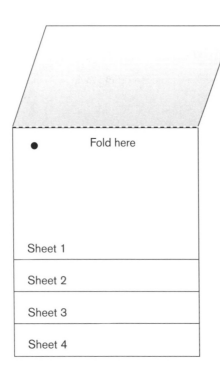

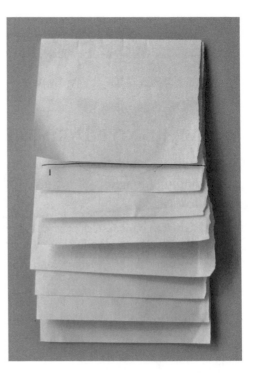

Figure 2.13

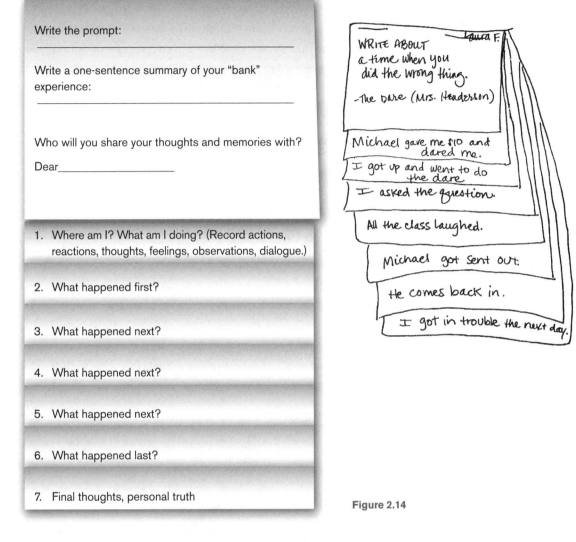

Write the prompt:

_____

Write a one-sentence summary of your "bank" experience:

_____

Who will you share your thoughts and memories with?

Dear_____

1. Where am I? What am I doing? (Record actions, reactions, thoughts, feelings, observations, dialogue.)

2. What happened first?

3. What happened next?

4. What happened next?

5. What happened next?

6. What happened last?

7. Final thoughts, personal truth

Laura F.

WRITE ABOUT a time when you did the wrong thing.
—The Dare (Mrs. Henderson)

Michael gave me $10 and dared me.

I got up and went to do the dare

I asked the question.

All the class laughed.

Michael got sent out.

He comes back in.

I got in trouble the next day.

Figure 2.14

7. I want you to read down your flips, from first to last. What do you notice?

8. Is there anyone whose flips _don't_ read like a summary of the experience? Can I look at what you wrote and see what happened?

9. Tell me three ways that the flipbook seemed to make writing _harder_ for you. Let's see what caused those difficulties.

10. Tell me three ways that the flipbook seemed to make writing _easier_ for you.

11. Tell me three things you noticed about your writing as you filled out the flipbook.

12. Tell me three things you now understand better about the flipbook—that you weren't sure about before we started talking.

13. Ask me three questions: anything about the flipbook that you want to ask.

Boosting the Odds for a Good Outcome

The main advantage of using flipbooks is the structure it provides for students' thinking and writing. You can supply additional structure throughout the process by making available to students the charts and rubric in Figures 2.15, 2.16, 2.17, and 2.18. The checks at each stage of the work provide concrete questions and expectations, and help give students valuable backup and specific goals.

Student Frequently Asked Questions About Flipbooks

1. **Why do we do the flipbook? How is it going to help us?**

   The flipbook is a way to organize an outline of your writing quickly and easily so that you can tell if it is complete before you begin to write. The pages in the flipbook keep the writer on topic for each event without jumping around.

2. **Why are there seven questions, and why do we do them?**

   The flipbook is a byproduct of the kernel essay, which has five questions. The flipbook has seven flips, so the kernel essay was expanded to match.

   We do the questions because their answers create a very simple, flexible writing path. It's easier to see the big picture clearly before you write. Without it, what you meant to write can quickly become entangled and lost in your off-the-beaten-path searches for the right word or that elusive detail.

3. **Do flipbooks make writing easier?**

   Yes, and this answer comes from the mouths of hundreds, maybe billions, of students who have told us so. They also tell us that it gets easier after you've done a couple.

4. **What are you supposed to write on the pages?**

   What you write on each page is the whole account of what the sentence on the flip has captured in just a few words.

5. **What if what you want to write about isn't an event, but just something you want to say?**

   I would suggest that you get your journal out and say what you want to say.

6. **What happens if we mess up with pen in the flipbook?**

   Your flipbook is your rough draft—in a book-ish sort of form. If you mess up, scratch it out and keep writing. If you're concerned about a scratch-out making it hard for you to read, then try using a pencil.

CAUSE: You didn't use the flipbook correctly

IF...	THEN...
You don't put the sequence of events with **actions,** *(not thoughts or feelings)* on your flips to organize your writing.	Your writing will become more and more vague and repetitive. You'll run out of anything to say.
You don't write "Where am I? What am I doing?" on the **first flip** so that when you begin writing, your FEET ARE ON THE GROUND inside the experience.	You don't know how to start, so your first paragraph is often vague and confusing. Then, you have a hard time getting started with writing the experience.
You don't set up your flipbook so that, page by page, you are *showing* what happened *next*—so that you can also show how you *reacted* to what happened next.	Your writing, by the third or fourth flip, will start to repeat. Since nothing new is happening, there's no new reaction . . . so you repeat what you've already said.
Before you started filling out the flipbook, you don't **figure out** and **write down** —on the FRONT COVER— what your **point** is for writing about *this* experience.	Your writing has no *focus*, no *undercurrent* of *purpose,* to guide it. After reading it, one could ask: **"Point? So what? Who's to care?"**
You convince yourself that the flipbook is a waste of your time. You set it up half-heartedly to please the teacher.	Your half-hearted flipbook leads to half-hearted writing that wanders confusingly from sentence to sentence.

EFFECT: Your writing becomes unfocused, confusing, vague, and repetitive. In a word: boring.

Figure 2.15: Cause and Effect (If . . . Then . . .) Chart

 Check our website for reproducibles

Self-Check: These Are the ABSOLUTE Requirements

Name_____Date_____

___1. I wrote the prompt down on the cover.

___2. I made a list of at least five experiences that show this.

___3. I wrote down what experience I chose to write about at the top of the back page.

___4. This planning lasted only fifteen to thirty minutes. No longer.

___5. I listed the things that happened (kernel essay) on the back of my flipbook.

___6. I moved that list to the flips on the front.

___7. I wrote *Where am I? What am I doing?* at the top of the first page . . . ONLY.

___8. I answered these two questions clearly before I wrote anything else on the first inside page.

___9. I am writing SIX OR MORE sentences on each inside page in TRIPLE SLOW MOTION, carefully connecting experience to the prompt.

Self-Check: These Are the ABSOLUTE Requirements

Name_____Date_____

___1. I wrote the prompt down on the cover.

___2. I made a list of at least five experiences that show this.

___3. I wrote down what experience I chose to write about at the top of the back page.

___4. This planning lasted only fifteen to thirty minutes. No longer.

___5. I listed the things that happened (kernel essay) on the back of my flipbook.

___6. I moved that list to the flips on the front.

___7. I wrote *Where am I? What am I doing?* at the top of the first page . . . ONLY.

___8. I answered these two questions clearly before I wrote anything else on the first inside page.

___9. I am writing SIX OR MORE sentences on each inside page in TRIPLE SLOW MOTION, carefully connecting experience to the prompt.

Self-Check: These Are the ABSOLUTE Requirements

Name_____Date_____

___1. I wrote the prompt down on the cover.

___2. I made a list of at least five experiences that show this.

___3. I wrote down what experience I chose to write about at the top of the back page.

___4. This planning lasted only fifteen to thirty minutes. No longer.

___5. I listed the things that happened (kernel essay) on the back of my flipbook.

___6. I moved that list to the flips on the front.

___7. I wrote *Where am I? What am I doing?* at the top of the first page . . . ONLY.

___8. I answered these two questions clearly before I wrote anything else on the first inside page.

___9. I am writing SIX OR MORE sentences on each inside page in TRIPLE SLOW MOTION, carefully connecting experience to the prompt.

Self-Check: These Are the ABSOLUTE Requirements

Name_____Date_____

___1. I wrote the prompt down on the cover.

___2. I made a list of at least five experiences that show this.

___3. I wrote down what experience I chose to write about at the top of the back page.

___4. This planning lasted only fifteen to thirty minutes. No longer.

___5. I listed the things that happened (kernel essay) on the back of my flipbook.

___6. I moved that list to the flips on the front.

___7. I wrote *Where am I? What am I doing?* at the top of the first page . . . ONLY.

___8. I answered these two questions clearly before I wrote anything else on the first inside page.

___9. I am writing SIX OR MORE sentences on each inside page in TRIPLE SLOW MOTION, carefully connecting experience to the prompt.

Figure 2.16: Student Self-Check Flipbook

 Check our website for reproducibles

Self-Check: These Are the ABSOLUTE Requirements

Name_____Date_____

___ 1. I am writing my final copy in pencil.
___ 2. I started writing on the first line.
___ 3. I am indenting each time I start a new page on the flipbook.
___ 4. With dialogue, when I change speakers, I am changing paragraphs.
___ 5. I am using quotation marks with dialogue.
___ 6. I am capitalizing the first words of quotations.
___ 7. I am not skipping a blank line between paragraphs.
___ 8. My handwriting is small, neat, and easily readable.
___ 9. I am not gapping between words.
___10. I am not forgetting to space between all my words.
___11. I am putting periods at the end of all my sentences.
___12. I am capitalizing people's names.
___13. I am capitalizing the word "I."
___14. I am writing as neatly on the back as I did on the front.
___15. My truism RELATES TO *THE PROMPT.*

Self-Check: These Are the ABSOLUTE Requirements

Name_____Date_____

___ 1. I am writing my final copy in pencil.
___ 2. I started writing on the first line.
___ 3. I am indenting each time I start a new page on the flipbook.
___ 4. With dialogue, when I change speakers, I am changing paragraphs.
___ 5. I am using quotation marks with dialogue.
___ 6. I am capitalizing the first words of quotations.
___ 7. I am not skipping a blank line between paragraphs.
___ 8. My handwriting is small, neat, and easily readable.
___ 9. I am not gapping between words.
___10. I am not forgetting to space between all my words.
___11. I am putting periods at the end of all my sentences.
___12. I am capitalizing people's names.
___13. I am capitalizing the word "I."
___14. I am writing as neatly on the back as I did on the front.
___15. My truism RELATES TO *THE PROMPT.*

Self-Check: These Are the ABSOLUTE Requirements

Name_____Date_____

___ 1. I am writing my final copy in pencil.
___ 2. I started writing on the first line.
___ 3. I am indenting each time I start a new page on the flipbook.
___ 4. With dialogue, when I change speakers, I am changing paragraphs.
___ 5. I am using quotation marks with dialogue.
___ 6. I am capitalizing the first words of quotations.
___ 7. I am not skipping a blank line between paragraphs.
___ 8. My handwriting is small, neat, and easily readable.
___ 9. I am not gapping between words.
___10. I am not forgetting to space between all my words.
___11. I am putting periods at the end of all my sentences.
___12. I am capitalizing people's names.
___13. I am capitalizing the word "I."
___14. I am writing as neatly on the back as I did on the front.
___15. My truism RELATES TO *THE PROMPT.*

Self-Check: These Are the ABSOLUTE Requirements

Name_____Date_____

___ 1. I am writing my final copy in pencil.
___ 2. I started writing on the first line.
___ 3. I am indenting each time I start a new page on the flipbook.
___ 4. With dialogue, when I change speakers, I am changing paragraphs.
___ 5. I am using quotation marks with dialogue.
___ 6. I am capitalizing the first words of quotations.
___ 7. I am not skipping a blank line between paragraphs.
___ 8. My handwriting is small, neat, and easily readable.
___ 9. I am not gapping between words.
___10. I am not forgetting to space between all my words.
___11. I am putting periods at the end of all my sentences.
___12. I am capitalizing people's names.
___13. I am capitalizing the word "I."
___14. I am writing as neatly on the back as I did on the front.
___15. My truism RELATES TO *THE PROMPT.*

Figure 2.17: Student Self-Check Flipbook Final Copy

 Check our website for reproducibles

Score Point 1	Score Point 2	Score Point 3	Score Point 4
Because of the way you have written this, it is too hard to read and clearly understand. There are problems with punctuation, spelling, proper grammar, and so on. There is also a problem with you repeating the same thing too much. It's hard to tell that you read the prompt and are focused on what it says. I didn't get the feeling, as I read your paper, that you really cared whether you did a good job writing or not. Let's work on that.	I can usually follow and understand the experience you are writing about—although there are places where I got lost. There are too many problems with run-ons, capitalization, and spelling. There are also problems with repeating and with this sounding more like a list of what happened instead of an explanation and showing of it. I often needed to reread and try to figure out what you had written . . . or what you had probably meant to write.	Your paper was basically clear from beginning to end. While there were some problems with correct punctuation and spelling, these did not keep me from being able to easily read and understand what you wrote. You shared your reactions and thoughts consistently. Some observations were uniquely exceptional. Your ending was clear and appropriate to your focus. If you had proofread (more) carefully, most of the errors could have been corrected.	Your writing captured me from the beginning. Where you were, I was. What you saw, I saw. What you thought and felt, I could understand and identify with. Your language skills added both clarity and meaning to your writing. My first thought when I finished reading your paper was, "Wow! I hope I can have a copy of this!" Thank you for taking the time and effort to produce writing of this quality.

Score Point 1	Score Point 2	Score Point 3	Score Point 4
Because of the way you have written this, it is too hard to read and clearly understand. There are problems with punctuation, spelling, proper grammar, and so on. There is also a problem with you repeating the same thing too much. It's hard to tell that you read the prompt and are focused on what it says. I didn't get the feeling, as I read your paper, that you really cared whether you did a good job writing or not. Let's work on that.	I can usually follow and understand the experience you are writing about—although there are places where I got lost. There are too many problems with run-ons, capitalization, and spelling. There are also problems with repeating and with this sounding more like a list of what happened instead of an explanation and showing of it. I often needed to reread and try to figure out what you had written . . . or what you had probably meant to write.	Your paper was basically clear from beginning to end. While there were some problems with correct punctuation and spelling, these did not keep me from being able to easily read and understand what you wrote. You shared your reactions and thoughts consistently. Some observations were uniquely exceptional. Your ending was clear and appropriate to your focus. If you had proofread (more) carefully, most of the errors could have been corrected.	Your writing captured me from the beginning. Where you were, I was. What you saw, I saw. What you thought and felt, I could understand and identify with. Your language skills added both clarity and meaning to your writing. My first thought when I finished reading your paper was, "Wow! I hope I can have a copy of this!" Thank you for taking the time and effort to produce writing of this quality.

Figure 2.18: Scoring Guide

 Check our website for reproducibles

7.   **What do we do if we need more room than the front and back of the page?**

First, examine your handwriting. Most of the students I know who write on the front and the back of a page and still don't have room to finish are writing too big. Write smaller.

If you are writing small, I would suggest that you read what you've written and decide if it was too big a chunk for one flip. Maybe you should divide it into two flips . . . or three. You can staple another flip on—or use a sticky note for more room.

But maybe, as you wrote, you discovered that this part was more meaningful to the whole experience—and deserved more consideration as you followed the movement of your mind—than you first realized. If so, follow your instinct. The worst you can do is screw up . . . and that's part of writing.

8.   **Do we have to answer the questions in full sentences?**

Have to? No. Does it help to? Yes, and here's why. When you answer the questions in sentences, it's very easy to sit back after you've finished your flips, read what you wrote, and see if it sounds right to you.

You can also do a quick check to see if you've committed any unpardonable crimes against good flipbooking (and, hence, against good writing). These include writing flip sentences that are:

>   not the answers to the kernel essay
>
>   not actions, but a thought or feeling
>
>   repetitious
>
>   confusing or illogical
>
>   unfocused—no point or purpose in sight
>
>   too vague to provide movement in your writing

9.   **Can we write about more than one thing?**

If by this you mean more than one experience, I would caution against it. Unless you have the writing ability to create an airtight, meaningful connection between "more than one thing," it's a much safer writing practice to stick with one.

10.   **Are we going to do a lot of these flipbooks?**

Success requires practice; practice requires repetition. We'll do as many as are necessary for success.

11. **Are we supposed to write the *questions* onto the flips?**

    No. You're supposed to write the questions onto your mind. Write only the answers to the questions onto the flips.

12. **On the back of the pages, can we add more "what happened next" questions?**

    If you need to, but on a cautionary note here: Have you chosen a topic to write about that is too big for the time and space you are being given? Or are you writing every little thing down instead of cutting to the chase and writing only what's important to illustrate your purpose for writing? You'll want to check.

13. **Do we have to fill up each whole page?**

    No, although students who are committed to writing well consistently do.

14. **Do we have to answer every question?**

    Yes. The answers to these questions create a solid framework for your writing. Poor workmanship in the framing of your writing can lead to poor quality of the end product. Would you skip a step in setting up the framework of a house— and trust that it would be strong enough to support all that it must? Probably not, if you planned to live in it. Likewise, to be alive within your writing, the security of a strong framework is necessary.

15. **Are the pages only about the sentences on the flips?**

    Definitely so! Extending/elaborating/expanding (call it what you will) the one sentence on the flip allows you to slow down and think instead of rushing off to whatever comes next. It lets you take the time to ask yourself important questions: What else should I say? What else is important? What else would make this clearer/better/more meaningful?

    The answers to these questions require time and space. The flipbook page offers you opportunity for both.

16. **How much time are we going to spend working on the flipbook?**

    Writing involves deadlines that teachers need to set and students need to respect. In our classes, we allow up to a week for completing each one of the first few flipbooks. There is much to learn about the possibilities it offers both students and teachers, and there are many confusions and questions that will arise, as with any new skill. But as always, the more you practice, the faster and better you get.

17. How do we start writing?

You begin on the first page of the flipbook—with the answers to the first questions. The hardest part is knowing where to go next, and that part is already done; the kernel essay takes care of that for you.

18. What do we do when we're done with the flipbook?

Once you're done, you'll recopy the whole essay onto lined paper. And while you're recopying, if you find yourself wanting to add things, you may. If you find yourself wanting to change things, you may.

19. Is this for a grade?

Yes. It takes a long time, so we give two or three grades on it. You'll get one grade when you get your kernel essay onto your flipbook; you'll get another grade as I walk around and see how much you've done. Are you working all period? That's worth a grade, too.

The Fake Flipbook

THE PROBLEM: *On the state test, students want to use a flipbook for their rough draft, but it is not allowed.*

THE SOLUTION: *Practice for two weeks prior to the test using a fake flipbook.*

■ How This Lesson Came About

The first year of using flipbooks, we approached the state test with confidence. "It's one milestone of many in your life," I told my students, "just another bump in your educational road. What matters most is that you have the tools to support your writing abilities. Use them on the test!"

A hand went up. "Ms. Candler, are they going to give us flipbooks to use?"

My heart stopped. How could I have forgotten to consider how they would transfer the support of the flipbook to a test where they wouldn't have one?

I watched their reactions as I told them they wouldn't have a flipbook to use. If they had moaned and whined about the unfairness of it all, I probably would never have taken the next step. But they didn't. They smiled demurely, casting knowing eyes at one another. I could just hear some of them thinking, *No flipbook? Great! I'll get through with the test even faster!*

Solutions sometimes surface before the problems they resolve even arrive. So it was then that I remembered my student Amanda, who had created her own flipbook one weekend when she'd lost the original that she still needed to complete. Taking two sheets of copy paper, she had folded them and drawn rectangles to use as flipbook pages. Then she'd drawn a line near the bottom of each to simulate the *flips.* She was off and running.

The next day in class, I handed out copy paper to each student, and we made Amanda-style flipbooks and did a mock setup of the kernel essay. (See the How-To Guide in Figures 2.19a–b.)

"Hey, it's an I-can't-believe-it's-not-a-flipbook flipbook!" one student said.

Another voice asserted, "No, it's a *fake* flipbook!"

And so the fake flipbook was born. That year, I watched as some students created a fake flipbook on the blank planning pages in their state test booklet. If there were only *some* in my room, I knew there were even fewer in other testing sites.

The students draw this "fake flipbook" on the blank pages of the state test booklet.	
This is the front cover of the flipbook. Students write the prompt, their personal "bank experience," the audience, and the point they want to make in their paper.	
	Flip 2 Put the answer to the second kernel essay question here: What happened first?
Students write in this box as they would on the first page of the flipbook, elaborating the answer to the first question of the kernel essay. They continue to use these large boxes as if they were the inside pages of a flipbook.	
Flip 1 Put the answer to the first kernel essay question here: Where was I? What was I doing?	Flip 3 Put the answer to the third kernel essay question here: What happened next?

Students continue writing in the large boxes as they did on the first page.	
Flip 4 Put the answer to the next kernel essay question here: What happened next?	Flip 6 Put the answer to the next kernel essay question here: What happened next?
Flip 5 Put the answer to the next kernel essay question here: What happened next?	Flip 7 Put the answer to the last kernel essay question here: What was the last thing that happened? Final thoughts.

Figures 2.19a–b: The Fake Flipbook How-to Guide

When we were able to get our hands on copies of the writing papers, we recognized that many other students had written from an internalized structure of the flipbook, even though they said they hadn't drawn one. That was good, but not good enough.

The next year, we did two rough drafts on fake flipbooks, which the kids drew themselves. It was the right thing to do. During state testing, throughout the building, fake flipbooks were filling up the test planning pages and transforming my students' writing. Give it a try, using the reproducible fake flipbook template in Figure 2.20a–b.

I've learned it's not about a test. It's about what helps my kids feel smart. It's about what helps them know they can *handle* a test. It's about what empowers them to organize their thinking and do their personal best.

The Fake Flipbook: Reproducibles

Cover	Flip 2 What happened first?
Flip 1 Where was I? What was I doing?	Flip 3 What happened next?

Figures 2.20a–b: Fake Flipbook Reproducible Template

Check our website
for reproducibles

The Fake Flipbook: Reproducibles (continued)

Flip 4 What happened next?	Flip 6 What happened next?
Flip 5 What happened next?	Flip 7 What was the last thing that happened? Final thoughts?

Figures 2.20a–b: The Fake Flipbook How-to Guide, *continued*

Check our website
for reproducibles

Student Spotlight: Esequiel

Esequiel was one of my seventh grade ESL students. He hated being in an English class. He preferred staring out the window to paying attention or working. In the hallways, he spoke Spanish to his friends. In class, he didn't speak at all.

Nor did he want to write.

When we wrote our first composition, he hastily scrawled six or seven lines as the deadline neared. When he saw his failing grade, he shrugged and returned to his window. Writing didn't matter to him; nothing I could say about writing mattered to him.

Then we began doing flipbooks, and something miraculous happened. He began listening to my instructions for the flipbook, fiddling with his multicolored pages as I spoke of writing about things that really mattered. He wrote and turned a page and wrote and turned another page, and he didn't stop until he had finished the flipbook.

I read his paper at home that night. And then I read it again and cried.

His erratic spelling and lack of sentence boundaries spoke of years of not caring, but the heart of his words stormed off the page with a hurt and confusion and anguish so *raw* that I felt like it was my own.

Here's his paper:

PROMPT: Write a composition about a time that someone hurt you.

He wrote about: *Somewon that mede me feal les of a person.*

(Students are allowed to scratch out the name of the person they're writing to if they don't want anyone to see who it is . . . and he did.)

Dear XXXXX,

I wa in lunch in a tabol with my friens having a good time eating owre food we were talking about how we felt of the T.V. Shows, and the persons in the T.V. We were just talking about original stuff. we were talking aboute times we gote in trobol, or almost got in trobol. You see we were havinng a good time until you came.

wen you came and sade all the harobol things you sade made me think that you were some kinde of resist or you were just taking your anger on somone. It wasent nise wat you sad to me because I wasen't wat you sade. waw thos wors wer strong the realy hurt all of the every singol one of them.

wen you sad all of thos things it hurt my fellings I thot I wasent a perso It made me feal like a dog or something that's not human a stupid nonhuman thing that no wan cares of. I felt so engry o you for telling all thos word I cant say in this paper but they weren't nice. You know how to hurt a guy like me with thos words.

I stayed quaet for the rest of the lunch time because I diren't dare to talke because I was embers and scared I thot I was going to loose my Friends because I didn't stand up for my self I thot that there were going to tell me that I was a chicken because of your folt. I felt like if the hole school went silent wen I wen silen I triyd not to crid and I accomplish it like my mom Says boy cry too.

I want you to lisen because wat you say is not nice no even to a dog becas it hurts feling. I have feling I'm almost the same like you because I have felings like you. Just imagin tha some one Says all of thos words to you around your friends, yore best friens you migth feal the same way I felt. No one in the world would like to here some one say that to them. I want for you to respect me.

That night I felt a desperate need to share Esequiel's paper with someone who would feel what I had felt when I read it. Someone who would see through the myriad of mistakes into the powerful *release* of truth and emotion that threatened to erupt like a volcano from within its walls of neglect and wasted potential.

I typed it up and e-mailed it to Gretchen Bernabei. I added a note explaining that the flipbook appeared to have simplified the writing process enough that Esequiel was able to say what he wanted to say without being overwhelmed by the sight of a blank sheet of paper.

Esequiel received his own copy of Gretchen's return email; her words of excitement and appreciation helped soothe something inside his troubled spirit. In time—after he took the only state writing test he had ever been eligible to take, after he started walking taller and holding his head higher in the hallways, after his attitude toward school had begun a reluctant blossom into willingness—he and Gretchen got to meet in person. They stood side by side in the foyer at my school, grinning hugely, as I snapped a picture of the two of them together. We both told Esequiel that if all men could articulate what he had, we'd have a better world. We, at least, knew that Esequiel's flipbook had changed so much more than just his writing.

And the test? He passed.

—CYNTHIA CANDLER

REVISION AND DEVELOPMENT

Cynthia's Story

Teaching has become a house divided, a constant tug-of-war between teaching to the test and teaching the subject. I realize this every time a new school year starts and the first thing people want to talk about is testing. I realize this every time I feel that as department chair I must teach my new teachers how to get our kids ready for the writing test. I realize this every time I attend a teacher workshop and the focus invariably turns to helping kids succeed on the test. Test prep is out there, too pervasive to be avoided.

But in the beginning was the simple act of teaching the writing skills students need to make it through life, to follow a dream. It bothers me that I can't look back over twenty years of teaching without gravitating immediately to the memory of trying to help my students become good enough writers to do well on the test. Maybe it bothers me because I remember being new and not really knowing how to approach teaching writing. And then someone put the state writing test in front of me and said teach them to do this, and I did.

That's probably how it happens for most of us. When we're too new to have developed our own hopes and writing goals for our students, someone says to make sure you get them ready for this one moment in the year. Our focus is reduced to a pinpoint.

I am only one of legions of writing teachers who have discovered that fear is a stern taskmaster—we fear having less-than-acceptable scores broadcast across the district, scores that are then dissected and scrutinized by any number of well-meaning individuals whose job it is to document every single place students have failed to meet state and national standards.

I always felt that the powers-that-be knew everything about my weaknesses and instances of failure and next to nothing about my successes. Truth is, they had information about my successes as well. But somehow the successes never seemed to be what mattered. The focus was forever on where I stumbled.

Another truth: I have a touch of "defiance disorder."

It was hard for me to remain committed to teaching to the test. I felt I had a leg up on the number crunchers: I had in front of me the flesh-and-blood students those numbers represented. I had an opportunity to teach these students something important, something that mattered, something that would help them get to places they didn't know they'd want to go.

By fits and starts, I kept returning to what I believed in most—that good writing was good writing, whether it was in a test booklet or a note to a friend or a paper for class. I knew that teaching good writing meant identifying the things students needed to know how to do, anticipating the problems they'd face, and exploring the possibilities for fixing those problems.

Lots of possibilities: There are many ways to begin teaching writing, a vast range of options for how to progress along the path once you've embarked, and much to be learned on the way to your destination. Of course, knowing this didn't change the fact that every year, come August, I would get jerked back to the reality of state testing.

Twenty years later, I remain in many ways where I was when I first began teaching. I make a writing assignment, watch my students trip over every pebble on the road, and try to get them back on their feet. I read their papers and make endless lists of things that aren't working. I forget I'm supposed to be scoring compositions and get caught up in a desperate attempt to find something that will work better for them than what they're doing.

I go back in on Monday morning and say, "Okay, this and this and this aren't working. What if we try things this way?" And they moan and look at me like I'm an alien. In their minds, what's done is done. In my mind, what's done is fodder for all the ways it could be done better.

My file cabinets are crammed with the evidence of my wandering in the wilderness of writing instruction. The many documents stored on my computer's hard drive offer mute testimony to my having returned again and again to try to fix the same problems.

Every year is the same, yet no year is ever the same. That's the paradox of teaching. It reminds me of the frightening ability of viruses to mutate to avoid annihilation. My kids' writing changes just enough each year to require that I examine with new eyes what I'm teaching them. Time and again I try a new focus, take a new direction, and, if I'm lucky, use new tools.

One comforting thing about teaching is that so many other dedicated people are in the trenches with us. In dire circumstances, everyone unites in the common goal of survival. If you want what I've got, it's yours. If you need a hand up, take mine. If you're scared, I'm here to tell you we'll be all right in the end.

Not long ago, I read one of my old teaching journals. The first entry was dated November 1995, six years after my first day in the classroom. Reading these long-ago words, I expected to discover how much my teaching had changed. What I expected to find wasn't there.

During those years I believed my students' problems with writing were my own fault because I didn't know enough about teaching to head them off or solve the ones I couldn't head off—it's the desert new teachers are convinced they are the first to attempt to cross. It would have comforted me to know I wasn't alone.

Here is some of what I was saying:

- *I am tired of telling kids simple things to do and having it be too hard for them to accomplish. When they write, they keep rushing through the story to get to the end. How do I convince them it's not about the end?*

- *Their writing makes me feel as though they have been out of touch with the lives they lead. Their focus is too broad—very, very broad—touching dozens of bases in one paper. But it's also very shallow, not touching anything in depth. Their attentiveness is to showing what happened without showing why it mattered.*

- *I need to find a way to teach them that detail is about showing what they see so they can figure out why it matters that they saw it. I don't know how to do that.*

- *I'm so tired of writing here about problems that never go away . . . how to get the students to write more specifically . . . what I need to do next. I can't see what I need to do next. And that scares me more than anything else.*

- *Faculty meeting today. Short day next Monday. Drug testing next Wednesday. What else, what else, what else will interfere with what I need to do? I don't even know what I need to do. How will I figure it out if they keep taking up all our time, if they keep taking my students away from me?*

- *I want my teaching back. I want to finish training these students for the test so we can get back to writing that feels good again. I want writing to feel like it is releasing something, to feel like it's satisfying something inside us.*

- *I told the kids that this will be an unfocused freewrite, but I think I was talking about myself. I am an unfocused freewrite. There's something grabbing at my guts—something whose shape is as blurred as heavy fog—something that is entirely difficult because I can't see what it is. I don't like being in the fog. I don't know if what's out there is safe or not, or if I'm even going in the right direction. I want to do something that will make a difference for my students. Something with a shelf life. Something that uses the gifts they've been given. This feeling inside me is eating itself because it's so empty and hungry.*

There it was—and there it still is: the truth of the journey. The searching I did, that we all do, for the best way to do things. Not the right way to do things, because there isn't one. Just the best way to teach real kids real writing and hope that what you're doing will pay itself forward through the rest of their lives.

Along the way, I've been privileged to meet other teachers who share the same hope. Their spirits and methods have invigorated my teaching. They have graciously given of their experience. They have offered me a hand up to new approaches. And because teaching has always been scary, they have reassured me—and countless others like me—that it will be all right in the end.

That's what this book is about.

CHAPTER 3

WRITING WITH STYLE

Expanding a Sentence: Revision Stations

THE PROBLEM: *The student has a kernel essay or a summary, and has no clue how to turn it into a complete essay.*

THE SOLUTION: *Using icons and questions as concrete guides, work on one sentence at a time to help the student "show, not tell."*

■ HOW THIS LESSON CAME ABOUT

"Can you add some dialogue?"

"But, Miss, nobody was talking."

We looked at that part again. *We went to the store, we bought some stuff for hamburgers, we went home.* Deciding to save the comma splices for another day, I stuck to the dialogue issue. Now I imagined Raymond and his mom at the checkout stand, wordlessly exchanging money for goods. Soon I had asked Raymond dozens of questions, and his dialogue took shape, spicing up the otherwise mute transaction and making his piece much more accessible to the reader. Of course!

The issue isn't how to get dialogue (or any other type of detail development) into a writer's piece. The issue is how to get students to ask themselves the dozens of questions that will lead to those details. Revision stations, discussed in "The Flipbook" Figures 2.9a–e, p. 39), are an ideal way to get that process going.

■ INTRODUCE THE CONCEPT

Before the lesson, choose one sentence from a recent personal experience to use as an example, and rewrite it ahead of time using the four Revision Station strategies, just to make the demonstration less time-consuming.

- Using an overhead projector or chalkboard, show a sentence of yours from a kernel essay. For example, *We went to the emergency room.* Explain that this sentence is like a skeleton, all bone. We're going to add to this to "flesh the sentence out."

- Ask "How would we add dialogue?" Demonstrate what talk you might hear right as that sentence was uttered:

   "May I help you?" "Do you think we're going to have to wait long?" "Look at how many other people are here." "His records are in your system; he was born here." "Let's go over here." "Do you want to sit down?" "Let's try sitting down." "He's heavy." "It hurts worse to sit down?" "And on Christmas night!" "It's all right, Julian." "Poor baby." "We're going to see the doctor in just a few minutes, and it will be all right." "Daddy's doing paperwork." "What do you think happened to them?" "I wonder if they have doctors nearby on Christmas night." "I bet they do." "I know it hurts, baby."

- Next, ask "How would we add thoughts?" Demonstrate.

   It's got to be broken. I wonder if they thought we abused him. I bet we'll remember this Christmas. Where did Johnny park? I wonder if Matilde's scared. I'm glad she's here. I didn't know this would happen. Babies heal faster than grownups. I'm so relieved that we're finally here at the hospital. I wonder if he'll ever be the same. Could he die? He slipped . . . on a paper box! Bucko's a little pale. I don't know if she can take this. One thing for sure . . . injuries on babies are horrible.

- Next, ask "How would we add images or things we saw with our eyes?" Demonstrate.

   Julian's face was contorted and his back was arched as I looked down at him, injured in my arms. His right foot was pointed in an unnatural direction. There were rows of chairs around us, mostly empty. One mom and her little girl sat staring at us with big eyes. I could see the open window leading to the receptionist, and my husband was leaning in toward the window, handing her a clipboard. I could not see any stretcher headed our way.

- Finally, say "Think about our senses. How would we add smells, sounds, the other senses?" Demonstrate.

   Julian's screams only paused when he drew in breath. His screams were getting weaker, though, because he had been screaming for so long. My fingers felt his little body tense up as he screamed again. "No!" he screamed. "Me hurting!" "My leg!" I heard Kim taking a deep breath next to me. We could smell the disinfectant they used. It all smelled like gauze and fear. Little

Christmas carols tinkled in the background. I could no longer taste the roast beef and mashed potatoes we'd had for Christmas dinner. Now I only tasted the harsh and bitter taste of what it means to be a grownup.

- Ask students to figure out a few questions that these sentences might answer. ("What was one thing you knew?" for example). Then show the Guiding Questions from the Revision Stations (see pp. 70–71).

- For the next step, ask students to take one sentence from their writing and try adding some answers from each category.

Debriefing:

1. How did that work out?

2. Did you find yourself wanting to tell what happened next? How did you stop yourself?

3. Did anyone have an easier time with one kind of expansion than another kind? Can you tell about that?

Variations

1. Amazing Speed Revision and Choral Reading

   Take one sentence for the whole class to work on. Split the class into groups of three or four and give each group sentence strips. Assign to each group one kind of revision. Set a timer for five minutes. The goal is to see how many sentences your group can write, using that one technique.

   When the timer goes off, have groups read their sentence strips. Mix the sentence strips up and post them on the wall, in scrambled order. Listen to them mixed up.

2. Revision Stations

   Put the Revision Station pages around the room or put miniature versions into the students' writer's notebooks (see Figure 3.1, "Elaboration: Where's the BEEF?"). Ask the students to provide the requested details and see what happens in their writing.

3. Color It Up!

   Distribute a "Keep Your Writing Colorful" sheet (see Figure 3.2) to serve as a reminder of the Revision Stations process. Start with a high-scoring student composition, and ask students to read it together with you, looking for all of the following:

   - Talking or dialogue (Highlight each example in red as you find it.)
   - Thinking or mental talk   • (Highlight in yellow.)
   - Seeing or clear images   • (Highlight in blue.)
   - Doing or action   • (Highlight in green.)

   Then invite students to find or create the same "colors" in their writing.

Elaboration–Where's the BEEF!!!!!!!!!!!!?
(Brain, Ear, Eyes, Feet)

 *What would your brain be thinking?*

 *What would you be hearing?*

 *What would you see?*

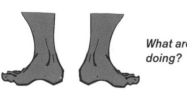 *What are your feet doing?*

Elaboration–Where's the BEEF!!!!!!!!!!!!?
(Brain, Ear, Eyes, Feet)

 Describe what your brain was thinking.

 Describe what you would be hearing.

Describe what you would see.

 Describe what your feet are doing.

Have students place a copy of this handout in their writing journal and in their homework folder for a quick revising guide.

Figure 3.1: Elaboration: Where's the BEEF?

Check our website for reproducibles

Figure 3.2: **Keep Your Writing Colorful**

Teacher Reflections: Four Tangible Results

✓ Students who participated in the "choral reading" of a group revision exercise could hardly believe how much they had written. "And it's good!"

✓ When hearing how many details a whole group could generate in just a few minutes, students voiced, "I'll never be able to get all that into the space I have." So instead of trying to figure out how to fill up their space, they're having to figure out what to choose from among all their possibilities.

✓ If you apply the color-coding idea to the highest-scoring papers from your state, you'll most likely see lots of mixed-up colors. If you apply the colors to the lowest-scoring papers from your state, you will most likely see only one or two colors.

✓ The students who used to need someone to ask them questions now have a tool to ask the questions themselves, and what they used to consider sheer brains and talent now looks like craft.

Guiding Questions for Revision Stations

Dialogue Challenge

- What did you say out loud?
- What did you whisper?
- What did someone else say?
- What did you say back?
- What did you stop yourself from saying?
- What did someone say under their breath?
- What voices were in the background?
- What did you hear them saying?

- What did you wish out loud?
- What song was anyone singing?
- What did anyone shout?
- What's one thing you're glad nobody said?
- What question did you ask?
- What answer did you get?
- What do you wish someone would have said?

Snapshot Challenge

- What was each person wearing?
- What expressions were on their faces?
- Where were they sitting? Standing?
- What was in their hands?
- What was the weather like?
- How much light was in the room?
- What could you see?
- What was in the background?
- What were people saying? Not saying?
- What were they about to say?

- What did you see? Not see?
- What were you afraid to see?
- What did you stare at?
- What caught your eye first?
- What did you see out of the corner of your eye?
- What amazed you? What did that tell you?
- What worries did you have?
- What did you *not* know about what you saw?

Sensory Details Challenge

- What smells could you notice?
- Could you smell any food smells?
- Could you smell any animal smells?
- What perfumes or colognes or soap smells could you recognize?
- What did the air smell like?
- What feelings could you smell in the air?
- What could you hear clearly?
- What could you just barely hear?
- What background noises could you hear?
- Did anyone's voice remind you of anything?
- What did your breathing sound like?

- Was there any music in the background?
- What noise did you expect to hear?
- What noise did you not expect to hear?
- What were you hoping to hear?
- What were you hoping not to hear?
- What were your fingers touching?
- What did anything feel like?
- Did the feel of anything remind you of something?
- What taste was in your mouth?
- What had you eaten recently?

Thoughtshot Challenge

Draw a stick figure with ten thought bubbles over the stick figure's head. Fill in the bubbles with thoughts you were having right then, such as . . .

- What did you know for sure?
- What did you wonder?
- What never occurred to you?
- What's one thing that you did *not* know then?
- What did you think when you looked around?
- What did you wish?

- What did you think would happen next?
- What did you think that other people were thinking?
- What did you believe?
- What did you tell yourself?
- What did you answer yourself?

■ STUDENT EXAMPLE FROM THE CLASSROOM

To expand his sentences, seventh grader Genaro Romero uses Spanish words in dialogue in this essay. Instead of directly translating, he alludes to the meaning of the Spanish in accompanying text. This is a technique that popular Hispanic authors (for example, Gary Soto and Sandra Cisneros) use in their published books.

Dear Chava,

"Hey, come on lets go to the lake," I asked you waiting for a responce. "Ok, lets go." We walked to the lake and started playing around with sling-shots. We shot cactuses and sometimes at birds. I saw a rabbit and thought we should get it, but we would have to chase it for a long time so I just kept on walking. We finally made it and decided to rest for a minute or two.

So we started running around looking for a good spot to rest and look at the lake. You found a good tree that had oranges with a good shade, so we decided to sit there. We sat there for awhile eating oranges and looking at the water. I stood up to pick another orange and then you said *"Mira!"* and pointed at the lake.

I turned around and couldn't believe my eyes. It was a humongous turtle. I told you if you get bit by a turtle it won't let you go until it hears a thunder or a donkey going "he-hong." So I told you just to leave it alone or you'll get bit. Like most times you didn't listen to me and stood up and said *"Vamos aggarrarlo."* But I didn't want to get the turtle but like always you didn't listen to me.

You started running to the lake and getting farther away from me because I was walking and because there were rocks in the way. When I got there you were kneeling down with a stick in your hand trying to pull the turtle close enough to get it with your sticky hands. I walked to you to help you get it, because your arm wasn't long enough. I tried but I couldn't do it either. I gave the stick back to you and then you tried again. You stretched and stretched. I thought your skin was going to pop off and then you stretched one more time and slipped.

"Splash!" I looked at you screaming and gulping water. I heard you screaming "Ayudame, no puedo nadar!" But the problem was if I jumped in to help you we'll both be drowning because I couldn't swim either. My choices were to run and get someone or stay there and watch you drown. "Ayudame!" I kept hearing you scream for help and it echoes through my ear out to my other ear and I still was watching you drown.

I wanted to help you so badly but for some reason my body froze, like a statue just watching you with a blank stare. "Man, I wish I could swim so I can jump in there and take you out." I looked around for a big stick but there was only twigs and grass so I couldn't help you in any way. I told you to try to grab my hand but you didn't hear me.

Your uncle and aunt were coming back from a store when they heard you screaming for help. They turned around and saw you struggleing in the water. They ran towards you and jumped in to get you out. I watched them take you out and make you breathe again. For awhile you weren't breathing, but then you coughed out some water and woke up.

When you did I, for some reason, started running away back to my house thinking why didn't I help you.

Genaro

Telling the Story, Asking Questions

(ADAPTED FROM After the End BY Barry Lane, ©1993, Heinemann)

> **THE PROBLEM:** *The student says, "That's all. I'm done," but the story lacks development and the student has no idea how to write more.*
>
> **THE SOLUTION:** *Telling their story and getting questions from the listeners gives students a tool for revising with relevant details.*

"Why would anyone believe that what they had to write was important if no one was listening to what they had to say?"

—Jayne Hover

■ How This Lesson Came About

Telling can be a vital part of writing for many writers. Some students are enthusiastic about telling their stories, but their written products show little or no excitement or development. Other students are weak writers because they do not have many opportunities to express themselves. For these children, writing exercises might be the only time that someone listens to them. If children do not feel that what they say is valued, why would they believe that what they put down on paper would make any difference?

This activity allows the students to build on their basic ideas. The focus is not on what is wrong with the paper but what can be added to develop and enrich the good writing found in each student. At times students already know something is lacking or not quite right and make comments such as, "I don't like my ending." Sometimes, when the best writers are stuck, the struggling writers come up with solutions. What a confidence builder!

Students will have different reactions to the prospect of telling their stories. Some will be thrilled and feel important; some will feel shy or embarrassed. The feelings of each student must be taken into consideration. The number one need of every human is to feel safe, and students must be able to trust that the classroom climate will make reading aloud and questioning a positive experience. It takes time to build enough trust for correction to be seen as helpful rather than destructive. Students should have options: They might prefer to write down their stories for sharing and questions; they might prefer to have the teacher or a classmate read their story aloud in the listening group; some might even want to tell their story to the teacher, who will then share with the group. Honoring those preferences will contribute to that climate of trust.

QUICK TIP: Be sure to remind students to tell their complete story and not leave out anything. Students may think they are supposed to leave things out because the model lesson left out some details.

■ INTRODUCE THE CONCEPT

- Share with students a short personal experience, leaving out the most intriguing details and cutting the ending short.
- Ask "Are there any questions?"
- Write down all student questions on an overhead transparency or chalkboard.
- Answer questions orally that the students have asked. Discuss with the class what they thought were the strengths of the story, and acknowledge the confusion of listeners who feel they were left with too many questions.
- Explain that writers often think they have written their story well, but readers may have important questions. The following activity will provide a way to hear what questions readers might have even before a story is written.

Practice Session

- In groups of three, the first student will tell his or her story as completely as possible.
- The two listeners will then write down three questions about the story that they would like answered and give them to the author. Encourage questions that require more than a one-word answer. The questions are not answered now but are put aside.
- The second and third students each tell their story and receive questions from the listeners.
- All students now return to their desks to write their story, including any information that might answer the questions they received.

Debriefing

1. How did you feel when you were telling your story?
2. Did telling the story help you remember more parts of your story?
3. How did you feel when you had to listen and come up with questions?

4. Was it difficult to find questions that took more than one word to answer?

5. How did telling your story and answering the questions you received help you write your story?

Variations

1. Have a willing student tell or read a story, and use the talking/questioning activity with the whole class.

2. When students have finished writing their stories, take turns with a partner reading stories aloud. Each listener will then write one "burning question" that absolutely must be answered and give it to the storyteller to aid in revising.

3. Writers will use the "burning question" or a question from the storytelling to write a new beginning or ending for their stories. Share the original and new beginnings/endings with others for feedback on which were the most effective.

4. Read aloud a picture book to the class and ask them to write questions that were not answered in the story, either as a class or in small groups.

5. Develop "what if" scenarios and new beginnings/endings of picture books or classic stories, and then write new versions.

■ EXAMPLES FROM THE CLASSROOM

MARIE: *A student's life is hard.*

QUESTION TO MARIE: *What makes a student's life hard? What do they have to do that is so difficult?*

MARIE: *A student's life is hard. Sometimes we get piles of homework, and if it isn't done, we dread the time it is due. We worry about what kids will act like. Kids wonder about their reputations, work, and demerits. I'm like that.*

KIYLEI: *"Hi. I'm Kiylei and I love throwing parties. Here's a time I threw a party for my mom. It was my mom's B-day she didn't want a big party but I did any way. I cleared up and put up decorations. Then I called up my mom's friends and we had fun. There was cake, ice cream, presents, and lots of games. When it was 4:00 p.m. everyone went home and my mom was happy."*

QUESTIONS FROM SALLIE TO KIYLEI: *What did you buy your mom and where did you get the money? How did you feel about your mom and the party? What was it like when you went to buy the gift for your mom? Do you like the beginning of your paper? What was the most exciting part for you?*

KIYLEI: *I stared at the wad of money in my hand with a grin. After 3 weeks of yard work it had all paid off. I could finally buy my mom a decent gift . . . (Kiylei's story went from there.)*

Katie: *She was bleeding.*

Question to Katie: *What part was bleeding?*

Katie: *She was bleeding from her knee down to her ankle. When I looked at it, it was about a centimeter deep.*

Student Reflections: Eight Heartfelt Testimonials

1. "It's better to say it first. It helps me a lot."
2. "You get to think about it for a while."
3. "Makes a big difference. It encourages us."
4. "I didn't have to think as much when I was writing because I already knew what I wanted to say."
5. "I like to write so much I may become a writer."
6. "I love writing. It makes me feel good. So good I don't even want to stop . . . I never knew I had it in me."
7. "I think writing is fun and cool."
8. "I think it's dumb but not as dumb as before."

The F.I.T. Chart

THE PROBLEM: *The student says, "I don't know what else to write. Do I have to write my whole story again?"*

THE SOLUTION: *Using the F.I.T. chart gives students an orderly and powerful way to write a story with more depth and detail the first time they write it.*

"Today I feel confident in myself. I am not scared about writing."

—FOURTH GRADE STUDENT

■ HOW THIS LESSON CAME ABOUT

One day my students were sharing their stories aloud with the class. When Abbie finished reading hers, there was a look of confusion on every face, including mine. As we tried to give compliments to Abbie, she sheepishly confessed, "I got a little confused myself. I left some things out of my story that I didn't remember at first, so I just put them at the end. Do I have to copy it over?"

"I think I know an easier way," I said. I pulled out my picture of Mr. Bean, Rowan Atkinson, and asked the group, "What do you think of Mr. Bean? Does he look strong to you?"

"No," they giggled. "He looks wimpy."

Then out came my picture of Arnold Schwarzenegger as the Terminator. "Do you think he looks strong?"

"Oh yeah," they chorused. "He's cool. He's tough. He's big."

"You know, sometimes our writing can be pretty wimpy, like Mr. Bean. But I'm going to show you an easy way to make it F.I.T. like Arnold Schwarzenegger. We're going to turn your writing from wimpy to wow. We'll use Abbie's story as an example of how to make our writing F.I.T."

I drew the chart in Figure 3.3 on a transparency for the overhead projector. Next, we took each of Abbie's sentences and put them in order under the Information column. "This is the outline for your story," I explained. "Look at the first item under the *I*. Think about it. What did you feel about that? Write that down under the *F* in the same row as the *I*. Did you think any thoughts when that happened, or did you say anything? Write that down under the *T* in that same line.

F.eelings	I.nformation	T.houghts (or speaking)

Figure 3.3: F.I.T. Chart

Now, look at each item under the *I* on your paper and ask yourself those same questions. If you had a feeling or thought about it or said or heard something, write it down on your chart. When you finish your chart, use it to rewrite your story." After trying F.I.T., Abbie read her story aloud again and the class applauded as she finished.

From then on, all I had to do was put my arms up in the air like I was flexing my muscles to remind my students to make their writing F.I.T. They loved the simplicity of the form.

QUICK TIP: Students should put only a word or phrase in the Information column. This keeps the activity from becoming too cumbersome.

■ INTRODUCE THE CONCEPT

Before the lesson, students will need an outline, kernel essay, or rough draft ready for this strategy.

Whole Class

- Put a transparency of the F.I.T. chart on the overhead projector.
- Ask students to turn their lined paper sideways (landscape) and copy the chart (or distribute the template in Figure 3.4).
- Say: "The *I* stands for information; this is where we write only the facts. Think about your story and ask yourself what happened first, then second, and so on. Write a word or phrase in the Information column until you finish your story." Allow students time to fill in the Information section of the chart.
- Say: "Now think about the first item in the *I* column. Ask yourself, 'How did I feel when this happened?' and write your feeling in the *F* column to the left. Then try to remember what you were thinking, or what you or someone else said at that time, and write it in the *T* column to the right of your first item."

F.I.T. CHART

Topic _____

Prompt _____

Truism (Life Lesson) _____

Check our website
for reproducibles

F.eelings	**I.**nformation	**T.**houghts (or speaking)

Figure 3.4: F.I.T. Chart Reproducible

Show the mock-up in Figure 3.5 to solidify the process in their minds. Continue by saying, "When you finish, ask yourself the same questions for the second item in your Information column, and fill in the Feelings and Thoughts beside it. Then complete the chart using the rest of the / items." (See the sample in Figure 3.6.)

- As students finish, have them share their F.I.T. chart with a partner. Discuss whether anything needs to be added, and then reverse roles.

- Students follow their chart as they write their story, being sure to include any feelings or thoughts as they write.

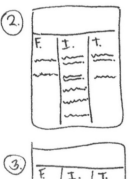

Figure 3.5: Mock-up of the
F.I.T. Chart Completion Process

FEELINGS ♡	INFORMATION	THOUGHTS.☁ OR DIALOGUE
We loved adventure and needed some.	There was a typhoon, strong wind — in Okinawa.	We called them hurricanes in TX— Remember Carla?
New feeling, thrill of exploring.	Water and hill description.	That hill was so high! We had never had such an opportunity.
Independence and curiosity— the "what if" excitement	Hank, Sue and I talked about the wind.	There's such a big difference between an idea and an actual experiment!
The pranky feeling Some soberness, a touch of fear	We strapped Sue onto a telephone pole to see if it would blow her sideways.	Could this be dangerous? How much wind would it take?
The feeling of ridiculousness crept over all of us— Lots of laughter	It didn't work. We watched her from lawn chairs. We came inside.	This was going to be a memory... haha!

Figure 3.6: Sample F.I.T. Chart

Debriefing

1. What do you think of F.I.T. as a way to write your story? Did anything surprise you?

2. How did the F.I.T. chart help you write your story?

3. Why is it important to have a balance of these things (feelings, information, thoughts)?

Variations

1. Have students tell their story as another student fills in the chart. Then the two students look over the chart to see if anything needs to be added before writing the story.

2. Have students brainstorm a story idea and use the F.I.T. chart as prewriting.

3. Encourage students to put the ideas in each F.I.T. row in different orders. Say: "Mix it up. For example, you might start with your information and then tell how it made you feel. For the next item you could start with your thought or what someone said, tell how it made you feel, and then give the information. You might decide not to use all parts of your chart, or to weave your feelings in with your thoughts. This is where you get to be creative and make your story come alive."

4. Students could highlight sentences in a rough draft with a different color for Feelings, Information, and Thoughts or Speaking to see if their story is balanced, then revise.

Teacher Reflections: Four Tangible Results

✓ *Students loved using the chart because they didn't have to write and rewrite their stories.*

✓ *This format works as both a prewriting and a revising tool.*

✓ *This strategy adds voice naturally for writers who use mostly information.*

✓ *It was easy for my students to add other lessons such as Ba-da-bing (p. 98) and truisms (p. 89) into the F.I.T. chart.*

■ STUDENT EXAMPLES FROM THE CLASSROOM

Abbie's Original Story

Trouble

When I got in trouble I was scared because I tore the skin off my little sister Hallie. Then she had to do it right back to me. But my arm wasn't as bloody as hers. And I was hurt badly me & Hallie got dinner early and went to bed at 8:00pm. The bad part was we share a room. I didn't go to daycare that day because I was hiding under my trampoline. And when my mom came home I got spanked. It I felt horrible.

Abbie's Revised Story

After using the F.I.T. Chart (see Figure 3.7), Abbie's story was much more complete and interesting.

F.eelings	I.nformation	T.houghts (or speaking)
mad	1. Hallie played with my favorite dinosaur.	That's my favorite dinosaur.
mad	2. I grabbed it.	"It's mine."
	3. She slapped.	
angry	4. I scratched.	I have a bad temper.
	5. Hallie told Mom.	
It hurt that Mom told her to do it back.	6. Mom said do it back.	I hear Mom tell her to do it back to me.
scared	7. Mom said after D.C., I would get spanked.	I have to hide.
	8. Went to D.C.	
Didn't want to be near Hallie.	9. Ran away from D.C.	
	10. Hid under trampoline.	
	11. Cruz found me.	
	12. Mom spanked me.	Not three but five times.

Figure 3.7: Abbie's F.I.T. Chart

Trouble

When I was at my house before daycare Hallie was playing with my toy dinosaur. That dinosaur was my favorite. So I snatched it from her and said, "It's mine," and then she slapped me. So I scratched my sister, but I didn't tell on her. I have such a bad temper. I didn't know what to do. I was only four. I heard my mom say, "Do it back." So she did it back. It hurt bad. Then my mom said, "After daycare you get three spankings." So when I was at daycare I said, "Can I go get a drink?" The teacher said, "Okay." But it was a fake drink because I lived so close, and I didn't want to be near Hallie. So I ran home and hid under my trampoline. But when my mom came to get us she realized I wasn't there. She said, "I know where she is." So she found me because of Cruz my dog. But instead of three, my mom spanked me five times.

Evan's Story

Evan's use of the F.I.T. Chart led to substantial detail that enhanced his story (see Figure 3.8).

F.eelings	I.nformation	T.houghts (or speaking)
Scared	1. Bikes fell over.	Wanted to run out of Toys R Us.
Funny	2. My brother Aiden tried to pick it up.	He is crazy.
Wanted to tease	3. He picked it up. It fell down again.	Wanted to laugh.
Wanted to help	4. His hand got stuck.	*His hand must hurt.*
I felt frozen. I couldn't move.	5. Mom came over there.	Oh, no, she is going to yell.
Yea	6. Mom helped Aiden get the bikes back up.	Phew, that was a relief.
Happy	7. They finished before the worker came to see what had happened.	Oh, no, I hope Mom and Aiden are done.
Scared because he got in the way	8. I zoomed right by Aiden.	If I hit Aiden I am dead.
Really mad	9. Aiden found a peddle car.	I need that peddle car.
Really happy	10. I found a police peddle car.	It's time to go to JAIL, AIDEN!
Sad because we were leaving Toys R Us	11. I want to go back to Toys R Us because I want to play with the police peddle car.	I have to come back here.

Figure 3.8: Evan's F.I.T. Chart

Crash! I quickly ran over to the bike room and saw my brother Aiden trying to pick up the bikes that he had knocked down. It was so funny I started to laugh. He tried to pick it up again, but they fell down again. I wanted to tease him. His hand got stuck. I wanted to help. His hand must really hurt.

Mom heard Aiden screaming, "Help, help," so she was coming. Oh, no, she is going to scream! But she didn't. She was helping Aiden. I thought phew, that was a relief.

She started to help Aiden pick up the bikes. I ran out of the bike room and saw a worker coming. I hope Mom and Aiden are done. They were finished before the worker came. I got on a bike and zoomed right past Aiden and thought, if I run over Aiden I'm dead! Aiden was running, and he found a peddle car. I need a car! As I was riding I found a police peddle car. I was really happy. I said, "It's time to go to jail, Aiden." When I had captured Aiden it was time to leave Toys R Us. I was sad we were leaving Toys R Us. I thought to myself, I have to come back here.

Sparkling Sentences

THE PROBLEM: *The student says, "I can't write" and stares miserably at the blank page.*

THE SOLUTION: *Sharing, discussing, and publishing their sentences help students believe in themselves as writers who then produce more confident and creative writing.*

"If you do not believe in yourself . . . chances are nobody else will."

—UNKNOWN SOURCE

■ HOW THIS LESSON CAME ABOUT

An enthusiastic lesson was in progress where the students were asked to think of a room they know well, list every detail they can think of about the room, then list any events or situations that occurred there. Choosing one event, students write down every feeling and thought related to that incident and then begin to write their story.

Aveion, an extremely shy little boy, drew the picture of his room, made a list of things in that room, but then just sat there, unable to put the first words of his story on his paper, saying "I can't write." Mrs. Long, a co-teacher, asked him, "Tell me about the bed. What makes it important in this room?" He replied, "The bed reminds me of the day of the incident." And his story took off.

He wrote:

> The bed reminds me of the day of the incident. She was lying down as sick as can be. We were having a party until my aunt yelled, "Larane!" Everybody ran to the room. All of a sudden everybody was walking slow. They started crying. I said, "What's the matter! What's the matter!" My grandmother died, my aunt, with tears in her eyes, sadly said. From that day on that room was off limits. It was only for memories.

The next day I wrote those closing sentences on the overhead and said to the class, "Listen to this," and there was a quiet gasp of awe. We discussed what was so powerful and "sparkling" about the sentences. The students poured out words of praise, and I recorded their comments beside the sentences. After copying the sentences and comments on butcher paper, I hung them on the wall. With that simple act, that writer came alive and so did his writing.

Our job is to convince children that they can write, and sometimes that means undoing years of unbelief. Finding Sparkling Sentences became a regular feature of our writing classes, and we posted them in our classroom and hallways. I was careful to make sure that every child eventually had a Sparkling Sentence on the wall. Sometimes all I could find was a wonderful choice of words, but I grabbed that and showed their work.

Every child can write a Sparkling Sentence. The students may not believe it, and it might take some work to find them, but they're there. And after displaying my students' sentences, seeing became believing . . . for all of us.

■ INTRODUCE THE CONCEPT

Before the lesson, have a sheet of large chart paper ready for class discussion and a sentence that made you laugh or grimace, a specific word that is just right for a situation, an unusual way to begin a sentence, or an effective aside.

QUICK TIP: This is one time when I write the sentences and comments myself rather than use student recorders. This keeps the focus on the content without any distractions.

Whole Class

- Draw a T-chart on a piece of large chart paper and title it Sparkling Sentences. Write a Sparkling Sentence on the left side, with the first name and last initial of the author, and record comments on the right side as the discussion progresses. Note: Ask permission from the student beforehand if you think it is necessary or if the story contains something personal. I always make minor corrections in spelling and punctuation that do not change the meaning in order not to embarrass students.

- Ask students what makes this sentence sparkle. Record comments as students share. Be sure to elicit specific comments that explain why certain words or phrases make the writing powerful and effective. For example, do not write: "I liked their word choice," but rather, "When they wrote *putrid,* it made my nose wrinkle."

- Post Sparkling Sentences prominently in the classroom and hallways of your school.

Debriefing

1. How did you feel when you saw your sentence on the overhead?
2. How did you feel when you heard the comments about your work?

3. How does discussing all these sentences help you in your writing?

4. How will you feel having your sentence published in our classroom and school?

5. What ideas have you taken away from our discussion?

Variations

1. Cut apart the sentences after they have been on the wall for a while and give them to the original author. Tell them that every time a little voice tries to tell them that they cannot write, they are to pull out that sentence and read it. They *are* great authors, and here is the proof!

2. Pass out "Permission to quote" slips and encourage the class to give other students permission to use the original Sparkling Sentence in their own writing (citing the original author, of course!).

3. Discuss Sparkling Sentences from books you are reading to the class or reading as a class.

4. Encourage students to find Sparkling Sentences in the books they are reading. Have them bring them to the literacy circle or writing circle.

5. Publish an anthology of Sparkling Sentences from the class. Let students discuss which sentences should be used and why.

6. Have students use the traits of good writing and show examples from the Sparkling Sentences for each trait.

7. Create Sparkling Leads and Sparkling Conclusions.

Teacher Reflections: Four Tangible Results

✓ *Students would read and reread their sentences and comments as long as they were displayed. The pride and joy on their faces was priceless. This activity was empowering to our writers. They showed more creativity and confidence in their stories and in their ability to write those stories. Students fed off one another with their writing. They came up with numerous ideas for their own work from reading other Sparkling Sentences.*

✓ *Seeing their work published changed many students' attitudes about writing; they couldn't wait to write. Creating a Sparkling Sentence became a conscious goal.*

✓ *As more and more Sparkling Sentences appeared in the hallways, other students passing through our halls stopped and read the examples. Teachers reported that students were inspired in their own writing because of them. This one lesson impacted the entire school.*

✓ *In March when we were allowed to read their state compositions, I recognized many of those Sparkling Sentences we had put on the walls. The sentences made sense and fit into the writing. I had to laugh.*

■ Student Examples from the Classroom

I said, "No, not going, not leaving." But do they ever listen to the kid in the red shirt? No! *—Bekah*

"Mmmm," I moaned as I took a bite of that big juicy burger. *—Marissa*

My friend may be messy, but he's my friend! *—Taylor*

Weeping, she fell on her knees in the soft grass of the forest and prayed. *—Marie*

"Sir, our Air Force has been taken down!" said one toy soldier. *—Isaiah*

He craned his neck to see a small hand holding him down. *—Fina*

I laid down, fell asleep, and called it a day. *—Patrick*

After a while I felt guilty, so I took the blame and got grounded. *—Rachel*

Fiona had no idea what she was doing. Everybody was going right, and she was going left. *—Kaley*

"Dang, this is harder than I thought," I told my sister. *—Christopher*

I wonder why the earth moves and we don't feel it. *—Gaby*

"What's this?" I asked as I picked up the mysterious cup. *—Rachel*

Her hair was soft and smooth, and her perfume smelled like cherry. *—Brandon*

What? You expect me to baby-sit on a Saturday! *—Joseph*

I could feel the air piercing my face. *—Preston*

The house behind us fell to the ground with a clatter. Tyler touched my ear and whispered, "Thanks, Buddy." *—Brandon*

"You still looking for a friend?"

"Ya."

"You're talking to him." *—Taylor*

Truisms with Picture Prompts

THE PROBLEM: *The students says, "I don't like my story," because even if they don't realize that their paper is shallow and boring, they know "it doesn't sound good."*

THE SOLUTION: *Using a truism or life lesson allows writers to connect their experiences to the world.*

"The difference between school and life? In school, you're taught a lesson and then given a test. In life, you're given a test that teaches you a lesson."

−Tom Bodett

■ How This Lesson Came About

I attended a workshop by Gretchen Bernabei where she showed us her CD of beautiful photographs called "Lightning in a Bottle." Each picture had a truism, or life lesson, which was used to teach students how to think deeper and to find insights into the world by developing opinions and creating bridges between their lives, the artwork, and their world. Even though some teachers were skeptical about using these lessons with elementary students (one even said, "My children don't have a world view. They're only ten years old."), I couldn't wait to try this with my fourth graders. We had so much fun. And the discussions! You would have thought that you were in a group of adults. The pictures sparked some of the deepest thinking I had ever heard from my students. My vice principal came in for a walk-through and the kids didn't even notice she was in the room.

We began discussing the truisms and photos often, making a collection of our favorite life lessons and finding ways to use them in our writing. When students would focus on the literal details of a picture, I'd just remind them, "Tell us what is true about life in general—for everyone—based on this picture." One day, while showing a photograph of the Vietnam War Memorial in Washington, D.C., I had the projector tilted so the truism wasn't showing at the bottom of the screen. Amid shouts of "Hey, we can't see the truism . . .," one student suggested, "Why don't you let us guess what the truism is?" The ensuing discussion absolutely blew me away. The students came up with: "Freedom doesn't come free"; "Some people risk their lives for people who don't"; "One person can change the future"; and many more. From then on, my class insisted on brainstorming our own truisms first to compare with the caption on the photo.

■ Introducing Truisms with Picture Prompts

(ADAPTED FROM "THE INSIGHT GARDEN" (PP. 54–55), *WHY WE MUST RUN WITH SCISSORS*, BARRY LANE & GRETCHEN BERNABEI, 2001, AND *TRUISMS* (PP. 2–9), *REVIVING THE ESSAY*, GRETCHEN BERNABEI, 2005, DISCOVER WRITING PRESS.)

MATERIALS: Photographs from Heinemann website, www.heinemann.com.

Check our website
for reproducibles

Modeling

1. Show a photo with the truism covered. Ask students to describe what they see.

2. Uncover the truism statement. Ask students what the statement means to them and how it connects to the photo. Ask if they agree with it and if they believe it to be true for almost all people.

3. Show and discuss more photos in the same manner. Explain: "We call these statements about life *truisms*. They tell us something that is true for almost everyone everywhere." *Verdad para todos,* in Spanish.

4. Show more photos, asking students to make up their own truisms, and then compare them with the truisms given to the photos.

Practice Session

• Show a photo and have students respond with truisms. Discuss with the class how a truism might be used to write a story, and where it might be placed (title, beginning, middle, end).

• Ask students to choose one truism and make a list of their life experiences that they could write about using the truism.

• Ask students to circle the experience they would most like to write about.

• Next ask students to draw a picture of the experience that they circled.

• Students now write for a period of time (suggested time: twenty-three minutes) based on their drawing, including the truism at some point in the story.

• Share stories as class listens to find the truism.

QUICK TIP: Students should experiment to find the best place to use a truism in their story. If everyone used a truism in their introduction, it would become "canned" writing.

Debriefing

1. Where did you use the truism in your story? Why did you place it there?
2. Do you think a truism makes a story more effective? What does it add?
3. How does a truism make you feel when you read it in a story?

Variations

*   Give a prompt. Ask students to jot down any personal experiences that come to mind from the prompt. Draw a picture of one idea/scene. Write several truisms under the picture. Write from the picture, and use one of your truisms somewhere in the story.
*   Read aloud papers that lack voice. As a class, find the main idea of the story and brainstorm truisms that might fit. Revise the paper, including truisms.
*   Look at sayings from well-known historical figures, such as Benjamin Franklin. Discuss why he might have made those statements. What was going on in history that might have caused Ben to say this?

Fun with Truisms

Where can you put a truism? At the beginning or at the end of the writing, definitely, but what about hiding them in the text? Holding a "hide-a-truism" contest in your classroom might produce a range of possibilities and a great classroom collection!

Show the students a few samples from movies or songs, like these:

*   The *Wizard of Oz* method: "Dorothy clicked her heels together three times, saying...<truism>."
*   The *Forrest Gump* method: "My mama always used to say, '<truism>.'"
*   The *Field of Dreams* method: (A voice only the character can hear, saying . . .) <truism>.
*   The *Gambler* method: "In his final words, I found an ace that I could keep, <truism>."
*   The *Lion King* method: "Never forget, my son . . .<truism>."

And when you see truisms embedded in ingenious ways, add these to your classroom collection, such as:

*   The Suzanne Deckert method: "I was at a hotel in Jamaica when I learned that <truism>."
*   The Lil Wayne *Prom Queen* method: "See you never know how . . .<truism>."

Teacher Reflections: Four Tangible Results

✓ *Students connect with truisms. A truism gives us the big picture. It brings us into the composition. We say, "Yes! That's true!" or "No! I won't accept that!" When we believe in something strongly enough, a truism brings those emotions into our writing. The reader finds himself nodding and agreeing or disagreeing but somehow making an emotional connection with us. It causes us to have a proprioception—a word young people absolutely love to use.*

✓ *It was surprisingly easy for students to transfer the truisms to their writing. Sometimes they could match a truism with a piece they were working on and then include it; other times a truism would remind them of a life experience they wanted to write about.*

✓ *When test time came, I was confident that my students had a bank of truisms that they could use with any prompt, and the results were astonishing.*

✓ *Using truisms in their writing elevated the students' work to a higher level of quality and allowed them to connect to something besides the prompt.*

■ STUDENT EXAMPLES FROM THE CLASSROOM

Writing Samples

Five student examples of fourth-grade writing that stemmed from or included truisms are provided in Figures 3.9–3.13 (pp. 94–97). The truisms the students used are identified with italics.

Truisms from Cynthia Candler's Classroom

1. I've learned that just because something is over, it doesn't mean it's gone, and I've learned that just because something is gone, it doesn't mean that it's away forever. *−Hailey Hull*

2. I've learned in life that you never know when the book ends. *−Kendall Whitfield*

3. Sometimes things have to happen. *−Trey Seddon*

4. I've learned that when you let your faith die, people are all around telling you not to bury it. *−Emily Bauer*

5. We may grieve for those lost on the earth while they rejoice on the surface of heaven. *−Audra Denney*

6. I've learned in life that saying goodbye is saying hello to the future.
   —Asia Garrett

7. Staring at your pencil gets you nowhere. *—Dominick Carr*

8. I've learned that nothing can actually stop you from doing what you want.
   —Isabel Guzman

9. Sometimes you have to climb a hill to find what you are looking for.
   —Kyri Ashby

10. I've learned that you won't be able to retype the bad decisions you made in your life. *—Chelsea Brown*

11. Sometimes the dreams that are far away are the ones you want to reach the most. *—Alan Dehtan*

12. I've learned that you have to look and think farther to find what you're looking for. *—Shanda Simpson*

13. Sometimes the things that sound and feel good turn out to be the worst.
    —Michelle Alford

14. Sometimes in life you don't get to live to see what you want to see.
    —Chriss Armendariz

15. I've learned you might have to let things go without saying goodbye.
    —Ambriel Hickman

16. I've learned it's always good to practice the thing you have to do.
    —Kim Grauer

17. Sometimes in life you just need a little help finding the right way to go.
    —Kamden Beistel

18. You can't kick your way out of everything. *—Ben Heisel*

19. Sometimes having a team is the next best thing to having a family.
    —Tamara Marsh

20. *To not care is to care. —Amy Kinjo*

21. Sometimes there's no way to know what's at the top until you get there.
    —Tierrani Noel

22. Sometimes the scariest, most painful things can be the most beneficial.
    —Anna Valdez

23. Sometimes you just have to take "Let's get out there and play" to a whole new level. *—Anna Valdez*

24. I've learned something that helps may hurt. *—Joshua Upton*

25. I've learned one person doesn't make a team. *—Joshua Upton*

26. I've learned that sometimes the pain is worth it. *—Hadley Neely*

27. Sometimes getting what you need isn't always fun. *—Hadley Neely*

28. I've learned that at the end of the day, mothers still love you.
    —Hadley Neely

29. Words are just as painful as shots. *—Kenoderick Wilcots*

30. Sometimes there is nothing to catch you. *—Alex Call*

31. I've learned that sometimes life isn't comfortable. *—Lane Smith*

32. Sometimes the fiercest animals can be soft. *—Alex Call*

33. Sometimes it takes a little scare to push you into doing something.
    —Daisy Ontiveros

34. I've learned that your parents will always question the path that you
    choose. *—Chelsea Brown*

35. Sometimes the path to the road to success is not always open; you have
    to clear the path yourself. *—Jasmine Cano*

36. Sometimes what is dead on the outside is alive in the inside.
    —Jasmine Cano

37. I've learned that what you choose in life is not always what you get.
    —Jasmine Cano

38. Sometimes your path is too dark to see. *—Tessa Cannon*

My Greatest Wish

by Fina

I wish that the hurt ones would not always find sadness in their lives. Soon that sadness becomes anger, and that anger can be very strong. In the end that anger was just a temptation of evil. It's like bitter sugar. Once it is in you, you do all kinds of things and once it is out you realize what you've done. A lot of times you find that your anger has hurt other people, and those people are angry, and then what you've experienced is what they experience.

I kind of wish there were no hurt ones. Your family should help you when you're feeling down, lost, or hurt. Have you ever heard "Home is where the heart is?" *Well, I think family is really where the heart is.*

Figure 3.9: My Greatest Wish (Fina)

My Greatest Wish

by Katie

The saying is "The world is a battle field" right? Well, what if it wasn't. If we didn't fight and argue like we do now we would have peace and get along and have a good life. To me all the wars and battles are hate. All of us have enemies, but we really shouldn't. My grandma says, "Life is too short to be fighting and arguing." I fight almost every 15 minutes with my sister, but I love her. Sometimes we do mean things to each other, and it hurts our feelings. It's a bad thing to do, but we let anger and frustration take over. It's how life is, but if we could get along, there would be peace. *Together we can change the world.*

Figure 3.10: My Greatest Wish (Katie)

Three Wishes

—Rachel

"I'm home," I yelled as I came into the house. I had just came home from school and was very tired. I went into the kitchen and got an apple to eat.

"I'm hungry too," said my sister Amber. She has asthma. Because she has asthma, she has to take a treatment every four hours and one in the middle of the night. I barely get enough sleep because her treatment is so loud.

"Give Amber a banana," my mom yelled from the washing room. Her name is Grace. I never get to see any of her family because its too far away somewhere in the Pacific Ocean.

As I gave Amber a banana I saw something out of the corner of my eye.

"What's this?" I asked, as I picked up the mysterious cup.

**Figure 3.11:
Three Wishes
(Rachel)**

(continues)

"My cousin Siyo gave it to me. She said that it was ancient in the family," said my mom. It looked like one of those cups on Aladdin that genies come out of. I rubbed the side and wa la! Out came a green, see-through genie.

"You are now able to have three wishes that will come true. You have 24 hours to choose them, and choose them wisely my friend, goodbye." I could not believe what had just happened, but if it was real, I liked it. The thing was, I had millions of wishes to choose from and all those things were stuff that I wanted. I wanted a lot of stuff, but my family needed a lot of stuff. My aunt had to go to Virginia from wherever she was, my sister had to get better, and my mom needed to be able to go to visit her family somewhere in the Pacific Ocean.

I went to my room to think about my decision. I went to my bed and thought and thought and thought.

"It's time for dinner," my mom yelled from the dining room. It's time for dinner already! I looked at my watch, and I had been thinking for four hours!

Dinner went by very slowly; every minute felt like an hour.

At school the same thing happened, I thought school would never end…but it did.

"I'm home," I yelled. I looked at my watch, and I had 5 minutes left! I thought for four minutes and fifty-five seconds. Five, four, three, two, one, all of a sudden the genie appeared.

"What are your three wishes?" he asked. I started to sweat and then said that I wished for my sister's asthma to go away, my aunt would come back, and that my mom would be able to see all of her family.

"You have learned a valuable lesson, and your wishes are now granted," spoke the genie. "I hope this lesson will help you in the future," and he disappeared. Five minutes later my dad came into the room.

"I got a raise, so now we can go to your mom's island! Your aunt was also found!" he said with excitement.

The next day when my sister went to the doctor, she was ok! *From that day on I thought of other people first. Moral: always care for others.*

Figure 3.11: Three Wishes (Rachel), *continued*

#1 Dad

—Kiylei

Bring! The school bell rang. "Oh no!" I yelled. I'm going to be late again. I ran to the classroom as fast as lightning. "Am I late yet?" I asked the teacher. "Not yet," she replied. I walked calmly to my seat when suddenly, BRING! The bell rang. It startled everyone.

"Okay class. Today we will be doing a project on your number one person." I was clueless about who to write about. I had a million different people to choose from. I raised my hand and asked, "Mrs. Fortune, how do we choose from a lot of people?" She kind of didn't listen, but I thought about the many people that had a grasp on my life.

That night I thought long and hard about what person was my number one person who was special to me. Just then it blasted into my head. "That's it!" I yelled. I finally had who to write about, my dad. I ran into the kitchen and asked, "Dad, what is it like in the army?" He kind of stared at me for a while and stood there. I got very impatient with him and asked again.

Well, the next day wasn't the best day, but at least I finally had someone to write about. I got to my classroom, and there was Mrs. Fortune just grading papers as normal. She was tall and had short, curly, blonde hair. She always wore one long powder blue polyester dress with her short high heels.

"Hi Kiylei," she said. I liked her as a teacher. She was very nice. "Are you ready for the project?" she asked.

"Not really," I remarked under my breath.

"What? I'm sorry I didn't hear you," she asked.

"Nothing," I swiftly answered. Ok so nothing was working out. As of now I had to think of something else before Friday or else.

I spent time with my dad to find stuff out about him. "Dad, where are we going?" I asked. We got into the car. He replied, "It's your choice."

Wow, I thought. It was my choice, and I chose the Rain Forest Café. He liked that thought. We got there and discussed all the stuff he does in the army and the things he likes and this is how my story goes:

My number one person is my dad. Why? Because he has done a lot of things for me, and he is fun to hang out with. My dad is a pretty laid back person and is serious when he needs to be.

He is in the army and does a lot of cool stuff like he has to jump out of airplanes and stuff like that. Oh, and did I say he is an E7? That's a doctor.

Figure 3.12:
#1 Dad (Kiylei)

(continues)

Most of all he makes me giggle a lot. And I guess I am a pretty lucky little girl. My dad is like my super hero, kind of like Super Man. To me he is not just another face in the crowd. He is different from everybody else. He has saved many lives, and if he wasn't here today I don't know what I would do without him.

So all is well, and people can go to sleep with no worries about getting hurt because my Super Man is on the way and keeping us safe so nobody will have to be scared about their loved ones getting hurt in battle. And as the saying goes, *"United we stand, divided we fall."*

"Oh yea!" I got and A+. I was so relieved that it was a good grade and not like an F or I would have been in a bad situation.

Figure 3.12:
#1 Dad (Kiylei),
continued

Stand Up for What's Right

—Abram

"Leave Kevin alone, Richard," I, Abram, yelled.

"Who's going to stop me, you?" Richard the biggest bully in the world laughed. Then he started to walk away still laughing.

"Why do you let him bully you, Kevin, you're my best friend so it makes me sad to see that," I tried to say in a comforting voice.

"I don't know," Kevin said in a winny voice then started to run for class. I ran too so I could try to help him. When I caught up with him he told me, "Please don't tell the teacher." Although I wanted to tell the teacher I respected his wish and didn't.

My mom picked me up from school at the end of the day, and I told her about Kevin. Mom said, "Try to get as many kids as possible to help you stand up for what's right."

"Ok. I will try that," I responded. When I got to school I waited until lunchtime to ask, and everybody said yes. After lunch when we went outside to recess. We saw Richard picking on Kevin. So we marched to where he was, and we all felt like soldiers about to go into war with a giant.

When we got to him I said, "Leave Kevin alone."

"I already told you that you can't do anything," yelled Richard.

Then everybody else yelled, "But all of us can."

"Fine," Richard said angrily, "I was getting bored with him anyway," and ran away.

Kevin came up to me and looked at me with a big grin then said, "I am the luckiest person in the world to have a friend like you."

Figure 3.13:
Stand Up for
What's Right
(Abram)

Ba-da-bing Sentences

THE PROBLEM: *The student says, "I don't want to change what I have already written."*

THE SOLUTION: *Writing Ba-da-bing sentences gives students an easy, powerful revising strategy that makes their writing come alive.*

"When you write real 'listy,' it means you don't like what you're writing about. It has to come from here," Sallie said, pointing to her heart. *"If you don't feel it, you won't be able to write about it."*

—SALLIE, AGE TEN, FOURTH GRADE STUDENT

■ HOW THIS LESSON CAME ABOUT

Students need to learn specific strategies to move away from basic informational writing. Gretchen Bernabei has developed a fun way to revitalize boring sentences, which she calls "Ba-da-bing" (*The Good Writer's Guide*, 2007). Students are asked to take one sentence, think *BA-* and add where they were, think *DA-* and tell what they saw, think *BING* and write what they were thinking. Revising one sentence at a time is not so overwhelming to students, and this effective tool adds voice and style quite naturally.

To introduce Ba-da-bing, I walk into class with a mop head (new!) on top of my head. I look at the students with a straight face and ask, "Why are you laughing? Do you like my hair? What are you thinking?" While recording responses on the overhead projector, I pass around the mop head and ask students to use all five senses to describe the scene with a word or phrase. Then I write the sentence, "Mrs. Hover walked into the room." and say, "Let's have each group create a sentence about this using a Ba-da-bing organizer" (see Figure 3.14).

| Where You Were | What You Saw | What You Thought |

Figure 3.14: Ba-da-bing Organizer

Examples that followed: "Mrs. Hover walked in slowly like an old grandma. She was wearing a funky hat that looked like alien spiders had taken over her head. It smelled like the sewer and I thought, she's finally snapped." "She slumped into the room wearing a ponytail-braided hat. It looked like a dog lying on her head and I thought, this is weird."

This is a different way of saying "Show me, don't tell me" that made sense to my students. We used every opportunity to Ba-da-bing. When our vice principal returned an errant student to the classroom, I asked them to write about it. "He came into the room." turned into "Right when he came in the room his eyes were flaming. He looked at me, and I thought, 'I'm toast!'" Students now eagerly tackled their own boring sentences with this concrete strategy.

■ INTRODUCE THE CONCEPT

Modeling

1. Walk into the classroom wearing something unusual (a funny hat, huge glasses, a big furry coat, and so on).

2. Ask students to jot down their immediate thoughts.

3. Pass around the item you were wearing and have students give one word to describe it; students may use any of the five senses, and words cannot be repeated.

4. Draw three large boxes on the overhead projector or board. In the first box, draw some feet; in the second, draw an eye; in the third, draw a thought bubble.

5. Ask small groups or partners to write a sentence describing your entrance that includes information from each of the three boxes: where they (or you) were, what they saw, and what they were thinking.

6. Share and discuss student group sentences.

Practice Session

1. Students now use their writing folders or pieces in progress to revise one or more boring sentences using the Ba-da-bing boxes.

2. Partners share and discuss before and after sentences.

3. Share with the whole group.

QUICK TIP: Ba-da-bing sentences are terrific to use as Sparkling Sentences. Be sure students use all three components.

Debriefing

1. What is the difference between the original sentence and the new one?
2. How does using the Ba-da-bing strategy improve the sentence? What do you notice about voice, word choice, and sentence fluency?
3. Where could you use this tool in your own writing? Do you think you might have some dead sentences in your own writing that you could bring to life?

Variations

1. Draw pictures or show photos and ask students to write Ba-da-bing sentences describing the situation.
2. Have students change the order of their Ba-da-bing sentences for creativity and individuality.
3. Write "Who-Am-I?" Ba-da-bing sentences in the voice of famous literary or historical characters. Ask others to identify the character.
4. Have students replace the eye in the center box with icons from other senses (ear, nose).
5. Change things up with "Ba-da-bang" or "Ba-da-boom" sentences. (See Figure 3.15.)

Teacher Reflections: Four Tangible Results

✓ *Ba-da-bing sentences moved writers from giving us just the facts to adding personality and genuine voice. Student writing came alive, painting a picture of the moment.*

✓ *The Ba-da-bing strategy adds depth by letting the reader inside the writer's experience.*

✓ *My students loved revising using Ba-da-bing sentences. Reluctant writers are willing to use this method because it is clear and easy.*

✓ *Students were proud of their revisions and gained confidence in themselves as writers. They could see the excitement and interest that these new sentences brought to their writing, and they could recognize the same elements in other writing.*

Ba-	Da-	Bang
Where you were	What you saw	–what you or someone else said
Ba-	**Da-**	**Boom**
Where you were	What you saw	–what physical sensation you had (for example, blushed, butterflies in stomach, sweating)

Figure 3.15: A Twist on Ba-da-bing Sentences

■ Student Examples from the Classroom

BEFORE: We went into Amanda's room. She threw the wet cookie up. It stuck there.

AFTER: We went into Amanda's room just as she threw the wet cookie up and it stuck there. I was thinking, "She is in so much trouble." —*Breanna*

BEFORE: I was scared.

AFTER: I took a step into the bus, saw a couple of scared kids. Ahhh! Watch out!
—*Chance*

BEFORE: The screaming stopped.

AFTER: The screaming stopped which I thought was funny because it just stopped when we heard the first "click" of the high heels and the custodian's boots coming down the hall. —*Alexis*

BEFORE: Suddenly, at the hallway to our classroom a streak of gray crossed the hallway.

AFTER: I was in the hallway when a streak of gray crossed like lightning, and I thought, Auggg! —*Fina*

Student Spotlight: William

It was August, and my fourth graders were excited about a fun lesson—writing a story about making something in their room come alive. They had laughed as I read a story about toys coming to life and enthusiastically made their lists of items in their bedroom.

"Can we make it up?"

"Yes! Use your imagination. What happens when you come to school? What do the things in your bedroom do all day while you are gone?"

This is my student William's story:

Wor

Da laygos wer fiteg da big toys. The big toys have win da battle but not the wor. Da laygos went in der hide but you ask wer in the dror day got spy cars with mochin guns and basycas dat true hot lava dey got dem and died who was left dey feitted laygos won and dye dem in da box and clen up der mes.

Looking at William's story of the fighting Legos, I knew I had a chicken-and-egg dilemma: what to do first—focus on the content of William's writing, or find a way to help him change the Spanish influence in his writing quickly?

William had been in a bilingual program in third grade where, according to William, "We read in English but never wrote in English." And here he was, in a "regular ed" fourth grade classroom.

Phonics seemed to be the answer, but it would require reinforcement at home. William's mother spoke very limited English and wrote even less, so I sent her an invitation to join her son, along with several other students, before school four days a week to focus on phonics. Her response: "Can I bring William's little brother [kindergarten] and his older sister [fifth grade]?" Why not?

Using flash cards, games, and PVC elbow pipe to better hear the sounds, my unusual tutoring group worked through all twenty-six letters. As time passed, more and more words became recognizable, and we could focus on the content. William's stories quickly became creative and longer as his confidence and mastery grew.

With a lightness in his step and grin on his face, William entered the classroom on TAKS (Texas Assessment of Knowledge and Skills) day. Head bent in concentration and pencil scrawling furiously, he seemed completely engrossed in his own world for hours.

Later, we were given our students' test compositions to read. Digging through the papers, I spotted the one I most wanted to read—William's essay titled, "The Mistical Animals." Creativity, enthusiasm, and voice wove through the piece. I jumped up from my chair and ran next door to show Carole, his other fourth grade teacher. "William passed! Look at his composition!" We celebrated like we had won the lottery, and we couldn't wait to share it with his mother.

Today William writes with joy and self-assuredness. He now has tons of words to use instead of the few he was originally bold enough to put down on paper. His mind is filled with stories, and now he has the tools to transfer those wonderful thoughts into written stories for all the world to read.

—JAYNE HOVER

William's composition:

The Mistical Animals

I'm tierd, I'm going to bed. It's cold in here thers the cover, boy is it warm. "Where am I?" "Could this be possible to be a dream?" I said.

Wow! I'm in a rainforest. Cool look at all the animals and insecs! Jagurs, butterflies, scorpions, spiders, snakes, and leaches and much much more.

What's thise, a poster it saies 75 million dollars if a red vinamos frog is capchurd.

Oooooo an adventure. Now where can the red vinamos frog be hiding. Croke croke well well what do we have here the red frog. Let me put my globs on gotcha! I got it, but then I felt sad.

By the way his eyes looked I just had to put him back in his straw home. I put a sign don't tuch animals law porpuse, or phase consacuenses by ruler of jungle.

But I wanted to see it one more time so I cheked they all turnd evil they chesed me out of my own dream. Aggggggggl, boy good fing that's a dream. "William!" "What" I said lets go to the jungle. Boy it's just the biging. Noooooo, why me.

CHAPTER 4

The Devil's in the Details

Great Beginnings

THE PROBLEM: *The student says, "I don't know how to begin my story."*

THE SOLUTION: *Give the student examples of what works and what doesn't.*

The blank page is an intimidating thing for most students. Getting those first words down on paper may seem impossible, even if they have a good idea for a story. *Where do I begin? How do I know what to tell first?* Here are some pointers for launching a story with a "great beginning."

DOS AND DON'TS FOR GETTING STARTED

First, discuss with students what *isn't* a good way to begin.

Remember *not* to:

1. Use the words of the prompt.
   "An important memory for me was when . . ."

2. Give away the most important part at the beginning.
   "One important memory was when my aunt died."

3. Talk to the reader.
   "This story is about the time I went to . . ."
   "I'm going to write about . . ."

4. Start in a time and place far removed from the action.

> *"I woke up in the hotel that morning . . ." (when your story is about an afternoon outing)*

Next, show students different ways to begin at the beginning of the experience.

Try one of these:

1. Show where you—and only you—are . . . and what you're doing:

> *"I sat on the steaming hot bench, eagerly awaiting the start of the game. I was slated to be the starting pitcher . . ."*

2. Start with an important line of dialogue:

> *"You know what? I am tired of this!" my momma yelled. "I'm leaving."*
>
> *"No, Mommy, no!" I screamed at my mom while she walked out to her car. "They're going to put him to sleep if you take him back."*

3. Start with this pattern: "I used to think . . . but then something happened . . ."

> *"I used to think that the people I loved would always be there for me. But then something happened, and I found out I was wrong."*

■ DRAW A PICTURE

> **THE PROBLEM:** *The student says, "I've written a whole page!" but the information is not important to the story.*
>
> **THE SOLUTION:** *Give the student examples of what works and what doesn't.*

Students frequently start their papers with information that is not relevant to their story. Discuss the problems and examples, and then have students draw a picture of their story.

Remember *not* to:

1. Start too far back–before the real story begins.
2. Start with the wrong focus–beginning with information not important to the story.
3. Start with too much confusing information.

Try this:

1. Draw a picture of your story showing the most important moment.
2. Don't go back in time. Start writing about where you were and what was happening at that very moment. Don't simply identify the scene and then move on.

   EXAMPLE: The author's drawing shows a backyard birthday party, but she starts her story hours before the action takes place.

   POOR BEGINNING: "It was a bright, hot sunny day. The day was November 13, 2005, the day I turned eleven years old. The first thing that happened, I had woke up and come downstairs . . ."

   GREAT BEGINNING: "My eleventh birthday party was perfect . . . for about ten minutes. All my friends were there, and the cake was sitting on a big table in the shade, surrounded by brightly colored gifts. Who could have guessed that this was the day the neighbor's dog would get loose?"

3. Look at your picture and focus on the most important part.

   EXAMPLE: In her picture, the writer shows herself reading the Christmas story to her family for the first time. Note how she loses her focus by talking about presents. Writing about the first time you read the Christmas story to your family is a one-of-a-kind story; writing about opening presents is not.

   POOR BEGINNING: "It was Christmas eve and we are about to open our presents from my grandma well all her Christmas presents on Christmas eve are pjs because she wants us to wear them that night. The morning of Christmas has arrived. We look in our stockings . . ."

GREAT BEGINNING: "On Christmas Eve, our family always gathers together to listen to my Dad read the Christmas story. It is a special tradition that I never thought would change. That year, though, as we took our seats around the tree, Dad said, 'Ashley, I think you're old enough to read the story this year.' My mouth fell open, and I could feel tears stinging in my eyes."

4. Write slowly, remembering details that are important to your main point. Including details that don't set a clear scene or move the story forward will just confuse your readers.

    EXAMPLE: In his picture, the writer clearly shows that his memory is about meeting a friend after he moved to a new town. However, he confuses us with too much unrelated information at the beginning.

    POOR BEGINNING: "It was about four or five years ago when it happened. I was over my grandmothers house and school had just ended. There was two more days left before we got out for summer vacation. I had it all planned out, but what I didn't know was that somebody else had made plans for me."

    GREAT BEGINNING: "How in the world was I supposed to have any fun this summer in a new town? It was already June, and the question had me pretty worried. Being the new kid in school, I didn't know many people yet, so when the boy from down the street showed up in my driveway with two fishing poles, a stuffed backpack, and a grin, I knew I was in for some summer adventure."

■ SHOW, DON'T TELL

THE PROBLEM: *Student papers frequently begin, "It was . . ." "I was . . ." "This was . . ." "One day . . ." and so on.*

THE SOLUTION: *Give the student examples of what works and what doesn't.*

Without realizing it, students often start all their papers with the same type of vague, general statements.

Remember *not* to:

1. Start compositions with the same generic phrases.
2. Include these phrases often, especially in the opening sentence.
3. Use variations of these phrases without recognizing them.

Try this:

Look at "Examples of General Beginnings" (Figure 4.1a) and discuss them with a partner or group. Then look at the more interesting revisions in "Examples Rewritten: Show, Don't Tell" (Figure 4.1b). Discuss the differences. Now rewrite the first sentence of your story in several different ways so that it will *show*—and not *tell*—the reader what is happening. Readers must see a picture in their minds of the place, the people, and the action from your words.

1. "One nice pretty day I was playing with my friends . . ."
2. "On December 13, 2005 I was sitting in class doing my work . . ."
3. "On one winter afternoon I was in south Texas hunting . . ."
4. "One day I was getting ready for school . . ."
5. "It was September 11, 2001 . . ."
6. "It was Christmas Eve . . ."
7. "It was four or five years ago when . . ."

Figure 4.1a: Examples of General Beginnings

1. "I threw the ball hard at Chrissy . . ."
2. "I looked at the topic on the English test . . ."
3. "My dad was sitting behind me in our deer blind . . ."
4. "I picked up my blue shirt and put it on . . ."
5. "The calendar on the wall declared that today was September 11, 2001 . . ."
6. "The Christmas tree was sparkling in the corner of the room . . ."
7. "The last day of third grade was only two days away for me . . ."

Figure 4.1b: Examples Rewritten: SHOW, DON'T TELL

Common Mistakes and Quick Fixes

> **THE PROBLEM:** *The student says, "I don't know how to improve my story."*
>
> **THE SOLUTION:** *Give the student examples of what works and what doesn't.*

■ COMMON MISTAKE #1: LISTING EVENTS WITHOUT DETAILS

Remember *not* to:

- Write too fast.
- Hurry to get finished.
- Just list what happened in order (what happened next . . . next . . . next . . .).

EXAMPLE: *"I was sitting in my room. My mother called me. She wanted me to wash the dishes. I told her I was doing my homework. She said to do them when I finished."*

Try this:

1. *Write* the first sentence in your story.
2. *Stop* writing.
3. *Read* what you wrote.
4. *See* the picture in your mind of what you're writing about.
5. *Think* what else is in the picture that the reader needs to know.
6. *Add* a sentence or two that might create a more interesting picture. *Tell* what people are thinking, feeling, or saying.
7. *Write* the next sentence from your story and *repeat* these steps for the whole paper.

EXAMPLE REVISED: *"I was sitting in my room listening to the new Alicia Keyes CD and writing a note to my best friend. The pink pen I was using kept spitting gooey blobs out on the paper. My mother's voice suddenly roared into my ears, over the sound of the music. "Katie, I need you to wash these dishes!" she screamed. I tuned her out; I liked the sound of Alicia better . . ."*

■ Common Mistake #2: Writing That Rambles On and On

Remember *not* to:

> tell *everything* that happened. Most of what *really* happened isn't important to the part of the experience you're writing. Including everything will only confuse or bore a reader. Decide what was important and write about that. Pretend the rest didn't happen.

EXAMPLE: *"It was a hot Saturday. Me and my family were in the backyard. My dad introduced me to my uncle. Then one day he came back to our house and we talked. Then we were going to have a family reunion, so we cleaned up the house. So the next day we got everything ready. Then everybody started coming. It was fun."*

Try this:

1. Figure out why you wanted to write about this experience. What was the one most important thing that happened that made you think of writing about this?
2. Cross out everything before that part and everything after that part.
3. Now, rewrite the one part slowly. Share your thoughts about what was happening and what you were feeling as it happened. Use dialogue.

EXAMPLE REVISED: *"I couldn't wait for our family reunion to start because my Uncle Jerry was coming. He lived in Arizona and I had never met him until he came to visit a few weeks ago. We sat in the hot backyard looking at my baseball card collection for an hour. We had been getting the house cleaned up for days, and now I watched every guest arriving hoping it would be Uncle Jerry so we could talk about baseball some more. 'Here comes Uncle Jerry,' my little brother shouted."*

■ Common Mistake #3: Repeating Yourself

Remember *not* to:

> repeat the same word, phrase, or idea over and over in your story.

EXAMPLE: *"One day in the middle of the night, I woke to hear my mom crying in the living room. I got out of bed and heard my brother and sister talking about what had happened. I went into the room to ask them what had happened. They said they didn't know. So we all went into the living room to ask her what had happened . . ."*

Try this:

1. Read your paper as you write it. Look for places where you are repeating.
2. Underline the repeated words, phrases, or ideas.
3. Rewrite these parts and get rid of the repetition.

EXAMPLE REVISED: *"One night I woke to hear my mom crying in the living room. I got out of bed, heard my brother and sister talking, and went into their room to ask what had happened. Since they didn't know, we quietly walked up to our mother to ask her what was wrong."*

■ COMMON MISTAKE #4: WRITING "BIG" INSTEAD OF "SMALL"

Remember *not* to:

- Use "big" general remarks (vague language) instead of "small" specific language to show what you mean.
- Think only about the big story idea and forget to examine that picture in your mind for details that set the scene or describe the action.

Examples of "big," vague sentences:

1. *My grandpa is really nice.*
2. *I did really great on my report card.*
3. *Jake's mother eats a lot of weird stuff.*

Try this:

1. Find the key word in your vague sentence—words like *nice, fun, stuff, good, great.*
2. Look "underneath" that word in your memory.
3. What's there? Why did you write what you did?
4. Add a sentence or two that shows what you mean after your vague sentence.
5. Or, rewrite the vague sentence. Neatly squeeze in a sentence or two that *shows* what you meant, instead of telling.

Examples of the above sentences with "small" details added:

1. *My grandpa is really nice. He takes me fishing on Saturday nights. He taught me how to bait my hook and always lets me tell my mom that I caught the biggest fish.*
2. *I did really great on my report card. When I got it, I could hardly believe my eyes. I'd made an A in everything except math.*
3. *Jake's mother eats a lot of weird stuff. He told me that she likes onion and pickle sandwiches and drinks her milk with a lemon in it.*

Preparing the Final Copy

> **THE PROBLEM:** *The student puts the last period on his paper, slams his pencil down, and says, "I'm finished!"*
>
> **THE SOLUTION:** *Give the student clear expectations that he has a non-negotiable responsibility to carefully reread the whole paper and correct all the mistakes he can.*

■ PARAGRAPHING

Remember *not* to:

> write a composition in one big, long, paragraph, because it gets confusing to read and looks immature.

EXAMPLE: *"I loved the way that one's fins were so colorful but I didn't want him to eat some of the smaller fish in my tank. That's right I'm picking new fish for my aquarium and I don't know what to get. We had just gotten to the Petco in Rockwall and I was amazed at the color some of the fish had. They had fish for saltwater and freshwater, but I was only looking for freshwater fish. I was really trying to find something that was really colorful but not very aggressive. The aquarium associate suggested guppies . . ."*

Try this:

1. Begin a new paragraph each time you change: location, time, action, person, dialogue, mood, focus, and so on.
2. Keeping in mind that you shouldn't paragraph every sentence, it is better to paragraph too much than too little . . . or not at all. Be sure you indent each new paragraph.

EXAMPLE REVISED: *"I loved the way that one's fins were so colorful but I didn't want him to eat some of the smaller fish in my tank.*

That's right. I'm picking new fish for my aquarium and I don't know what to get.

We had just gotten to the Petco in Rockwall and I was amazed at the color some of the fish had. They had fish for saltwater and freshwater, but I was only looking for freshwater fish.

I was really trying to find something that was really colorful but not very aggressive. The aquarium associate suggested guppies . . ."

■ PROOFREADING

Remember *not* to:

> turn in your paper without correcting common mistakes.

Any of the problems listed here will result in lost meaning and/or confused readers.

1. Word/words are left out.
2. Letters are left out.
3. Writer puts in the wrong word.
4. Sentences don't have any punctuation.
5. Words are spelled wrong.
6. Paragraphs aren't indented.
7. Dialogue doesn't have quotation marks.
8. Corrections are written over the mistake, instead of the mistake being erased and rewritten.

Try this:

1. Place a dot on your writing sheet in the margin on every fifth line.
2. When you reach each dot, stop and reread what you have written.
3. Correct mistakes.
4. When you finish writing, reread the whole paper and correct anything you have missed.

■ HANDWRITING

Remember *not* to:

> turn in your paper if it contains any of the following:

1. Handwriting is too big or too small, sloppy, or illegible.
2. Words have big gaps between them or not enough space.
3. Letters are loopy, swinging from the top to the bottom of the lines.
4. The letters *i* and *j* have bubbles over them instead of dots.

Try this:

1. As you begin a new composition, write the first few lines of your paper.
2. Stop and look at your handwriting.
3. Ask yourself if you have any of the above problems.
4. If so, erase two or three words at a time and rewrite. Continue with good handwriting.

Remember, good handwriting is:

1. Neat and easy to read.
2. Dark enough to read.
3. Spaced appropriately between words.
4. Consistently good from beginning to end of paper.

CRUNCHTIME TOOLS AND MINILESSONS

Jayne's Story: Teaching Writing or Teaching Testing?

"Can you teach writing?" asked the principal sitting across from me.

I thought about the handwriting lessons I had taught in private schools. I was so good at making sure every *i* was dotted and every *t* was crossed. I could spot a misplaced loop from a standing position.

"Yes! I've had several years of teaching writing," I answered with a confident smile.

"Great. Then you're just the person we're looking for."

I was thrilled. My first public school job and fourth grade was one of my favorite grades to teach, but all too soon my world would begin to tilt.

Conversations would begin, "What grade will you be teaching?"

"Fourth. Isn't that great?" I still could hardly believe my good fortune.

"Oh. Fourth." I'd catch a look of pity. "And you are excited about fourth? You don't mind the writing?" Why the look of concern? Well, I'd think, I guess not everyone enjoys teaching handwriting.

"No, of course I don't. I taught writing for years in private school. I know how to teach writing."

"So, you don't mind that composition they have to write in February?"

Silence. Composition? What was she talking about? "What composition?"

"The state test. You know, the one- to two-page composition they write in February."

I couldn't admit that all this time I'd thought I would be teaching handwriting, not composition. All the worried looks, all the strange glances began to make sense. I suddenly realized just how naïve I was. I didn't know anything about teaching *that* kind of writing.

From the talk in the teachers' lounge that fall, I learned that a 4 on a composition was the best score, and a 1 was not passing. That's it. That represented the depth and breadth of my knowledge of compositional writing. Oh, and handwriting didn't matter much.

About the third week of school, an experienced fourth grade teacher handed me some posters with letters and numbers, like I-4 and P1-5.

"Use these for the writing," she advised.

Seeing the confused look on my face, she continued, "The students number the lines on their paper. Then they follow the layout on these posters. Their introduction should be four lines, first paragraph five . . ." My head started spinning. They number the lines on their paper? Their introduction must contain four lines? *This* is how to teach writing?

She was still talking. " . . . so, their composition should have seven paragraphs, including the introduction and the conclusion. Put these posters up where they can see them and memorize them," she finished with a flourish.

Politely, I took the posters to my room, looked at them once more, and then relegated them to my closet. I didn't know what I was supposed to do, but clearly this couldn't be it.

I had to start somewhere. As I faced the students sitting in their chairs staring at me, I decided to begin their first writing exercise by gathering some information.

"What do you think about writing? Please be perfectly honest. If you love writing, tell me why you love it. If you hate it, tell me why you hate it."

As I sat on my couch that evening reading their folded slips of paper, I realized I was not going to get much help from the students. Their insecurities and frustrations matched mine. For example:

"I hate thinking of ideas to write down. And I don't like writing it."

"I kind of like writing. I don't like writing a lot because it takes too long to write a whole page of words, and it hurts my hand when I write too much on paper."

"I feel nervous because I think I will get a low grade. I think the teacher will not be able to read my handwriting." (Now *this* child, I could have helped!)

I didn't feel confident in my own writing skills, so how was I going to teach these students? Surely, there was something out there that made sense. And then, in a most unlikely place, I found it.

Finally getting a long overdue haircut at Phillip's salon the following Saturday, I began visiting with a wet-haired lady sitting next to me, also a fourth grade teacher. Trying to sound like I knew what I was talking about, I casually asked, "So, how do your students do on the state writing test?"

"Oh, they get mostly 4s and 3s, occasionally a 2."

What? Did I have shampoo in my ears? How did she do it? I had to know more. Was I going to have to go back and dig those posters out of my closet?

With eyes sparkling, she continued, "I use barilane."

"What's a barilane?"

She smiled, and I could tell I had just pushed that "I-can't-wait-to-share-this-with-you" button that every teacher has. "He's a person, Barry Lane, and he has the best books on teaching writing." The enthusiasm in her voice as she explained strategies like "thoughtshot" and "snapshot" and "looking through binoculars" was contagious. Here was someone talking about actual writing activities with purpose. And with scores like that, who could argue?

As soon as I paid for my haircut, I drove straight to Barnes & Noble and bought their only copy of Barry Lane's *After the End*. This was the first time I had read a professional book for teachers that read like a novel. I couldn't put it down. I kept reading parts out loud to my husband, Jim.

"This book is hilarious. And it makes so much sense."

After the fourth or fifth interruption, Jim grinned at me and said, "I think you found what you've been looking for." The next day, after using Lane's "Telling the Story First" lesson, I announced, "You only have seventeen minutes

to write. Ready, set, go!" My students looked like runners lined up for the 100-yard dash.

When the allotted time was up, I said, "Put your pencils down. Stop writing."

"What? Do we have to stop?"

"I want to write more. Can I write more than just a page?"

"Can I take my story home to finish it? There is more that I want to write."

"Do we have to go to P.E.? Can't we stay here and write?"

Did they just ask to skip P.E., the highlight of their day? I stole a glance at Candy, my co-teacher. We both stood there stunned. She was as dumbfounded as I was.

All the way home, I thought about that class. Students asking, no, *begging* to continue writing. And that was just the beginning.

As the year progressed, we incorporated more authentic writing activities, and each lesson yielded wonderful responses. I was not sure what was more fun—watching the students learn to love writing, or falling in love with it myself.

Maybe because I was as inexperienced as the students, together we discovered how to talk about our writing with one another. I asked them for help with my writing, and they asked each other, not just me. We were in this together, cheering each other on. I remember the first time Stephanie shared a wonderful piece that read as a complete story, instead of her usual disconnected thoughts and ideas.

"Stephanie, that was terrific!" The spontaneous applause from the class turned her cheeks the shade of pink lemonade. As I looked around the room, I realized they weren't just applauding Stephanie. They were cheering because they all had a part in her success. Now, it was not just me saying, "You gotta hear this!" The students were saying it, too—to me and to each other.

As the weeks went by and the fun continued, it was easy to forget that February loomed on the horizon. But questions hung in the back of my mind like a heavy curtain ready to drop down at the end of a wonderful play. What if the state did not like the type of writing the students were doing? What if I had left out things that should have been covered? Students' writing folders overflowed with chunks and pieces and a few completed compositions, but what if the more experienced teachers were right and they needed more *form* to their writing? I knew in my heart that the students loved to write, but what would happen on the day of the test?

Then real voices joined with the imaginary ones in my head.

"What you are doing may be fun, but will it work for the real test?"

"I really think you should go back to the formula writing. We know this works with our children. We've always had high scores using this method."

I shared my insecurities and my defiance with my most trusted colleague. "Candy, we may be totally off the mark for the state test, but you see how excited they are, right? I like what I see in these kids—the enthusiasm and love of writing. I don't know how they will do on that test, but I am willing to take the chance. These kids love to write. I have confidence that we have done the right thing."

There would be no last-minute changes. The test came and went, and the scores came back. Candy and I held our breath—and our methods were validated. The school writing scores were in the high 90s, beyond anything we'd expected.

For the next few years, I continued to build my arsenal of authentic writing activities using what I had learned from Barry Lane and working with others in my city, like Gretchen Bernabei. Gretchen and I exchanged ideas, and I joined our local NCTE affiliate to get more ideas. My students did well at test time, and my confidence as a writing teacher grew.

But then came the year of the crisis, and the bottom fell out.

Six weeks before the actual state test, our school's fourth graders took the previous year's release test as a benchmark. Of our six fourth-grade classes, two classes had over 50 percent failing compositions.

I could picture those classes. One had spent five months on grammar worksheets. Yes, the teacher of the other class had worked hard, but things had not come together. The results showed that only 69 percent of our fourth graders had passed the writing benchmark test, with an additional 14 percent barely passing. Our school had always scored in the 90s, and when I saw the results, I knew we were in trouble.

I approached our administrators with a plan: Could our grade level take four mornings for the next five weeks and concentrate on writing, dividing students into groups based on their benchmark scores and giving them targeted lessons for their specific needs? They agreed.

Group 1 was made up of the thirty-five students who failed the benchmark test, along with the seventeen additional students who barely passed. Group 2 would be made up of the forty-seven students who solidly passed. The remaining group would be made up of the fifteen students who achieved a high score on their paper.

At this point, we had only five and a half weeks before the actual test. Would it be too little, too late? I didn't know, but we had to try. For the next five weeks, we focused on writing four mornings a week, using lessons and activities like those you see in this book, three-and-a-half hours a day. Not only did we see our most reluctant writers produce, but something happened to our grade level: There was a camaraderie among the teachers that I had never experienced before. Joined in our common goal, we cried together, laughed together, and worried together as we watched our students' progress.

After five weeks, the students took the state test. An incredible 97.5 percent passed. Out of the original group of fifty-two struggling writers who seemed destined to fail, only four did not pass on the actual test. Students who achieved the rating of commended performance, which requires a score of 3 or 4, went from 13 percent to 44 percent.

A breakdown of the results is shown in Figure A.

"Tell me. What do you think about writing now?" I asked my group of former reluctant writers. A few of their responses follow:

"I love writing. It makes me feel good. So good I don't even want to stop.

I ended up improving at everything, even spelling . . . I never knew I had it in me."

"It makes me feel like Dr. Seuss, always wanting to share and express yourself and get all the ideas out of your head."

"You get to express yourself. I came a long way . . . I feel like I am an author."

That's why I'm sharing my story. It's the "hairdresser" phenomenon. I picked the brain of the teacher sitting in the chair beside me in the hair salon one day. After some success, people began picking my brain, asking how we went from 69 percent to 97.5 percent passing in five short weeks. Now we are passing our methods for success on to you.

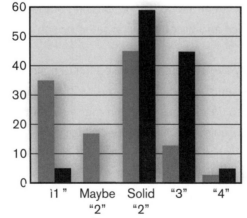

	"1"	Maybe "2"	Solid "2"	"3"	"4"
Release Test	35	17	47	12	2
Actual Test	4	0	59	45	5

Figure A: Comparison of Release Test and Actual Test Scores

COUNTDOWN TO THE TEST

KISS (Keep It Surprisingly Simple): The Concept

Figure 5.1 offers an outline of a four-week unit designed to give students sustained writing practice, different prewriting structures, tools for revising, and an audience for their work.

Lessons have been planned for four days a week, in sixty-minute periods. Students will spend the majority of the class periods writing after introductory or mini-lessons. There are assigned prompts for two of the weeks, and students will choose their own topics the other two weeks. They will have four completed writing pieces at the end of the unit.

We recommend that teachers return to these writing activities again and again after the state assessment. The short-term goal may be meaningful test preparation, but the long-term goal is even more significant—to build and equip *lifelong writers.*

WEEK 1		
Monday	Make class WRITER'S TOOLBOX chart	30 minutes
	Introductory TRUISMS lesson	30 minutes
Tuesday	Minilesson "The Bunny Escape" on sensory words	15 minutes
	Write a KERNEL ESSAY	45 minutes
Wednesday	Discuss more photos and truisms	10 minutes
	Write compositions	50 minutes
Thursday	GREAT BEGINNINGS, SPARKLING SENTENCES	15 minutes
	Write final copy, share with partner	45 minutes

WEEK 2		
Monday	Share and discuss TRUISMS	10 minutes
	Make QUICKLIST, fill out "A Memory" TEXT STRUCTURE	50 minutes
Tuesday	Minilesson "A Time to Help" on dialogue	15 minutes
	Write a rough draft of essay, skipping lines for revising	45 minutes
Wednesday	Introduce and share BA-DA-BING SENTENCES	15 minutes
	Write compositions, revising to add Ba-da-bing Sentences	45 minutes
Thursday	Read aloud two or three essays, compare Quicklists to common prompts	15 minutes
	Write, edit, and proofread final copy	45 minutes

WEEK 3		
Monday	Write a KERNEL ESSAY	20 minutes
	Transfer Kernel Essay to FLIPBOOK	40 minutes
Tuesday	Minilesson on "Ironing" on layering thinking	15 minutes
	Expand flipbook by writing inside pages	45 minutes
Wednesday	Minilesson on using REVISION STATIONS	20 minutes
	Rotate through Revision Stations	40 minutes
Thursday	Read aloud samples, post Sparkling Sentences	10 minutes
	Write final copy	50 minutes

WEEK 4		
Monday	Minilesson "Mittens" on blending sentence functions	20 minutes
	Write Kernel Essay, use "The Story of My Thinking" structure	40 minutes
Tuesday	Share and discuss TRUISMS	10 minutes
	Minilesson on Common Mistakes, finish rough draft	50 minutes
Wednesday	Model using Let's Get F.I.T. chart	15 minutes
	Copy rough draft onto F.I.T. chart	45 minutes
Thursday	Minilessons The Final Copy	10 minutes
	Write final copy, proofread	50 minutes
Friday	CELEBRATION!	60 minutes

Figure 5.1: KISS Lesson Plan

 Check our website
for reproducibles

KISS Lesson Plans for Writing

■ WEEK 1

(See Week 1 outline in Figure 5.2.)

Monday

1. Make a large class chart called Writer's Toolbox to be displayed during the unit (see Figure 5.3). Place tool icons down the left side, and brainstorm with the class which strategies students know or have been taught already (such as similes and metaphors, strong verbs, onomatopoeia, and using the senses). Write each strategy next to a tool icon on the chart, and write an example under the name. Add new strategies as they are learned. (Thirty minutes)

2. Introduce Truisms. Write the truisms (life lessons) on a large poster or butcher paper as the class discusses the "Lightning in a Bottle" photos or those the class has compiled, and have students keep a list of their favorites in their writer's notebook. Ask students how the truisms might fit in stories, essays, or compositions that they have written so far. Keep the Truisms poster displayed in the classroom, adding to it as students generate more during the unit. Add truisms to the Writer's Toolbox chart. (Thirty minutes)

Tuesday

1. Minilesson on sensory words (see "The Bunny Escape," p. 130). Add Sensory Words to the Writer's Toolbox chart. (Fifteen minutes)

2. Prompt: "A Time I Helped Someone" (or similar). Using the kernel essay with an example of your own, model how to write an outline by answering the kernel essay questions on the overhead projector. Students will then

WEEK 1		
Monday	Make class WRITER'S TOOLBOX chart	30 minutes
	Introductory TRUISMS lesson	30 minutes
Tuesday	Minilesson "The Bunny Escape" on sensory words	15 minutes
	Write a KERNEL ESSAY	45 minutes
Wednesday	Discuss more photos and truisms	10 minutes
	Write compositions	50 minutes
Thursday	GREAT BEGINNINGS, SPARKLING SENTENCES	15 minutes
	Write final copy, share with partner	45 minutes

Figure 5.2: Week 1 Outline

write the outline of their story with markers on large construction paper. (Varying paper choices seems to help keep student interest.) Next, students will read their outline to a partner who will check to see if it makes sense, tells the whole story, or includes anything that should be left out. Partners may ask questions for the writer to answer if there are confusing parts. (Forty-five minutes)

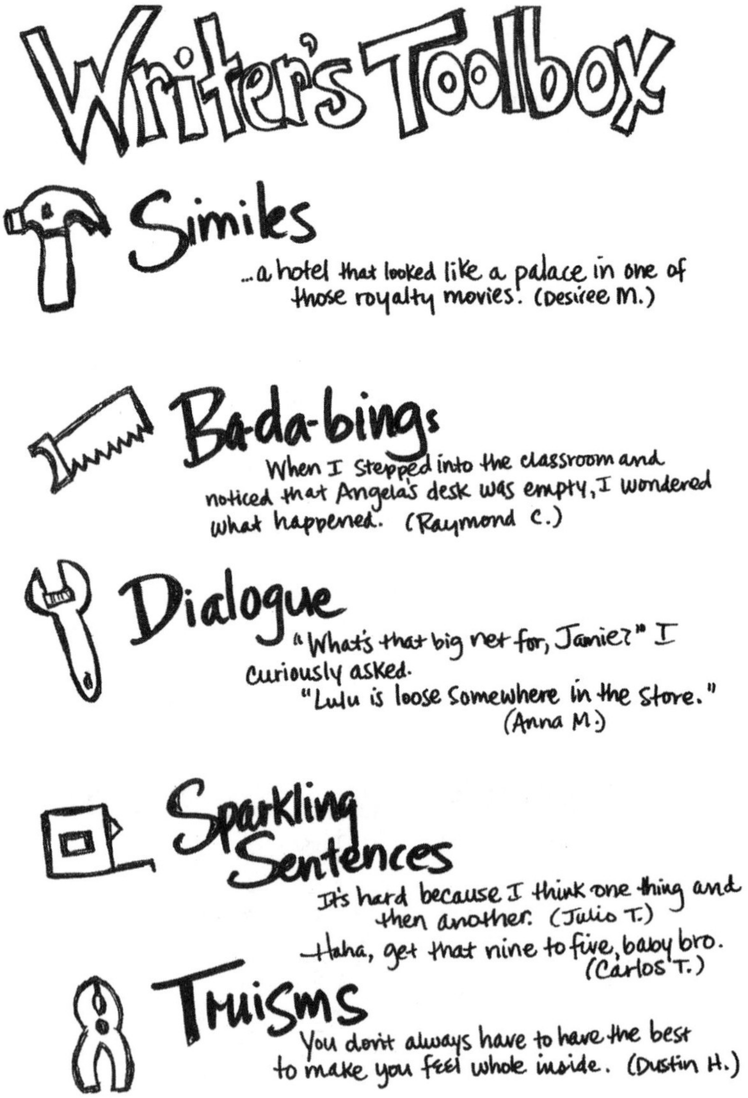

Writer's Toolbox

Similes
...a hotel that looked like a palace in one of those royalty movies. (Desiree M.)

Bada-bings
When I stepped into the classroom and noticed that Angela's desk was empty, I wondered what happened. (Raymond C.)

Dialogue
"What's that big net for, Jamie?" I curiously asked.
"Lulu is loose somewhere in the store."
(Anna M.)

Sparkling Sentences
It's hard because I think one thing and then another. (Julio T.)
Haha, get that nine to five, baby bro.
(Carlos T.)

Truisms
You don't always have to have the best to make you feel whole inside. (Dustin H.)

Figure 5.3: Writer's Toolbox

Wednesday

1. Show more photos, discuss the truisms, and add them to the class chart. Encourage students to think about where they could place a truism in the story they are going to write. (Ten minutes)

2. Students will now write a composition from their kernel essay on lined paper. Tell students that some Sparkling Sentences from their stories will be shared with the class the next day. Students will be motivated to write Sparkling Sentences that might be chosen for display. (Fifty minutes)

Thursday

1. Minilesson on Great Beginnings from the Flipbook minilessons (p. 104). Select good leads or other Sparkling Sentences from student essays and read these aloud. Write them with student comments on paper on sentence strips, using the author's name, and post in the classroom or hall. (Fifteen minutes)

2. Students will write a final copy of their composition and read aloud to partners as they finish. (Forty-five minutes)

■ WEEK 2

(See Week 2 outline in Figure 5.4.)

Monday

1. Share and discuss a few more photos with truisms. (Ten minutes)

2. Guide students through Making a Quicklist, then introduce "A Memory" from Structures with Kernel Essays (p. 29; see Figure 5.5). Students will select a topic from their quicklists to use with this text structure. Model while having students write a sentence or two for each box. This becomes their prewriting. (Fifty minutes)

WEEK 2		
Monday	Share and discuss TRUISMS	10 minutes
	Make QUICKLIST, fill out "A Memory" TEXT STRUCTURE	50 minutes
Tuesday	Minilesson "A Time to Help" on dialogue	15 minutes
	Write a rough draft of essay, skipping lines for revising	45 minutes
Wednesday	Introduce and share BA-DA-BING SENTENCES	15 minutes
	Write compositions, revising to add Ba-da-bing Sentences	45 minutes
Thursday	Read aloud two or three essays, compare Quicklists to common prompts	15 minutes
	Write, edit, and proofread final copy	45 minutes

Figure 5.4: Week 2 Outline

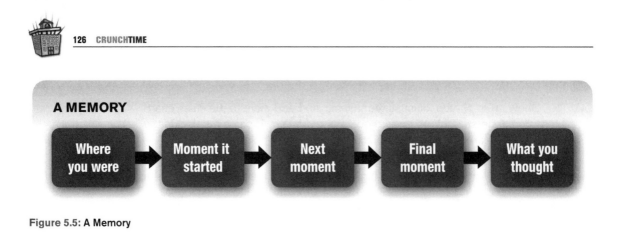

Figure 5.5: A Memory

Tuesday

1. Minilesson on dialogue (see "A Time to Help", p. 132). Add "Dialogue" to the Writer's Toolbox chart. (Fifteen minutes)

2. Students will write rough draft on lined paper, skipping lines for later revising. (An ideal choice is the old dot-matrix computer paper, the kind with alternating white and green lines, if you can find it.) Remind them to incorporate dialogue and a truism. (Forty-five minutes)

Wednesday

1. Introduce Ba-da-bing sentences and brainstorm examples with the class. (Fifteen minutes)

2. Students will finish rough drafts and revise by adding Ba-da-bing sentences. Have students revise in color—this makes it fun and also helps the teacher to identify and assess the revisions. Bright-colored map pencils work fine, and colored pens or gel pens are especially appealing. Almost everyone will want to revise! (Forty-five minutes)

Thursday

1. Read and discuss a few student essays, finding and posting more Sparkling Sentences. Discuss how students' quicklist topics could match a variety of open-ended, generic prompts. (Fifteen minutes)

2. Students will now write a final copy, editing and proofreading for mechanics and usage (with partner, if time permits). (Forty-five minutes)

■ WEEK 3

(See Week 3 outline in Figure 5.6.)

Monday

1. (Have a flipbook prepared for each student in advance–see directions, p. 43.) Have students write a kernel essay for the prompt "A Time I Learned Something New" or "A Time I Learned a Lesson." (Twenty minutes)

2. Introduce the flipbook by reading aloud an example of a completed flipbook, and tell students that they will be writing this week's composition as a letter to the person who taught them something. Guide students through placing their kernel essay on the front and back of the flipbook (see directions in "The Flipbook," p. 37). (Forty minutes)

Tuesday

1. Minilesson on layering thinking in a letter (see "Ironing," p. 133). (Fifteen minutes)

2. Students will now fill in the inside pages of their flipbook (see directions in "The Flipbook," p. 38). (Forty-five minutes)

Wednesday

1. Introduce Revision Stations (see p. 39 and the minilesson, p. 130). Review "Ba-da-bings" and "Sensory Words." Explain "Snapshots" and "Thoughtshots" carefully, if they are new strategies to students, and add to class Writer's Toolbox chart. (Twenty minutes)

2. Students will now rotate through Revision Stations to find sections in their flipbooks to expand using these tools. Use the Guiding Questions (see p. 70). (Forty minutes)

WEEK 3		
Monday	Write a KERNEL ESSAY	20 minutes
	Transfer Kernel Essay to FLIPBOOK	40 minutes
Tuesday	Minilesson on "Ironing" on layering thinking	15 minutes
	Expand flipbook by writing inside pages	45 minutes
Wednesday	Minilesson on using REVISION STATIONS	20 minutes
	Rotate through Revision Stations	40 minutes
Thursday	Read aloud samples, post Sparkling Sentences	10 minutes
	Write final copy	50 minutes

Figure 5.6: Week 3 Outline

Thursday

1. Read aloud one or two flipbooks from students whose work has not been heard yet, discussing and posting more Sparkling Sentences (p. 84). The goal is to have every student's work shared or displayed during the unit. (Ten minutes)

2. Students use their flipbooks to write a final copy of their letter on lined paper. (Fifty minutes)

■ WEEK 4

(See Week 4 outline in Figure 5.7.)

Monday

1. Minilesson on blending sentence functions (see "Mittens," p. 135). (Twenty minutes)

2. Introduce "The Story of My Thinking" from Text Structures with Kernel Essays (p. 31; see Figure 5.8). Have students choose a topic from their quicklist, write a kernel essay, and begin their rough draft. (Forty minutes)

Tuesday

1. Share and discuss a few more photos with truisms. Write these on the Truism class poster. (Ten minutes)

2. Discuss Common Mistakes and Quick Fixes from the Flipbook minilessons (p. 109) with the class. Remind students to be on guard for these as they finish writing, rereading, and revising their essays. (Fifty minutes)

WEEK 4		
Monday	Minilesson "Mittens" on blending sentence functions	20 minutes
	Write Kernel Essay, use "The Story of My Thinking" structure	40 minutes
Tuesday	Share and discuss TRUISMS	10 minutes
	Minilesson on Common Mistakes, finish rough draft	50 minutes
Wednesday	Model using Let's Get F.I.T. chart	15 minutes
	Copy rough draft onto F.I.T. chart	45 minutes
Thursday	Minilessons The Final Copy	10 minutes
	Write final copy, proofread	50 minutes
Friday	CELEBRATION!	60 minutes

Figure 5.7: Week 4 Outline

TRUISM: *You can find adventures anywhere in life*

THE STORY OF MY THINKING

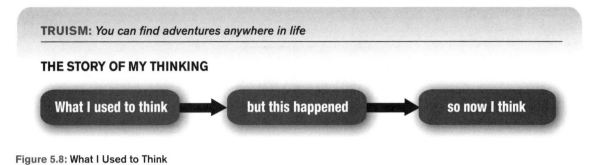

Figure 5.8: What I Used to Think

Wednesday

1. Model using the Let's Get F.I.T. (p. 78) chart on the overhead projector. (Fifteen minutes)
2. Students will now analyze their work by writing their essay on a F.I.T. chart. Students then revise to add some of the kinds of sentences that would make their story more balanced, and cross out any sentences that do not belong. (Forty-five minutes)

Thursday

1. Discuss expectations using The Final Copy from the Flipbook minilessons (p. 49). (Ten minutes)
2. Students will now write a final copy that meets class standards for paragraphing, proofreading, and handwriting. Students who finish may work with a partner to check mechanics. (Fifty minutes)

Friday

Celebration! (Sixty minutes)

Choose one:

1. Have a variety of copy paper with fancy borders available. Students choose their favorite composition from the unit to write or type on decorated paper. "Publish" on a classroom or hall bulletin board.
2. Have each student read aloud their favorite essay in a whole-class sharing circle.
3. Have small groups of students read aloud their favorite essays to each other.

MINILESSONS WITH
HIGH-SCORING STUDENT PAPERS

Anna Matthias, *The Bunny Escape*

**Check our website
for reproducibles**

Type of Minilesson: Sensory Words

Writers don't use every strategy they know all the time. They pick and choose whatever works best for each situation.

Anna treats her readers to a masterful flurry of noise, not from beginning to end, but just when the story truly gets noisy.

ACTIVITY:

- Read the piece.
- Highlight the words and phrases that bring sounds to a reader's imaginary ear. Notice where those words and phrases are concentrated.

Examples: thrash, squeaking, squawking, screeching, crowing, whistling, whispered.

CHALLENGE: Find (or build) a moment in your own writing where there's a sensory flurry. Add enough sensory words so that a reader's imaginary senses feel it.

The Bunny Escape

Anna Mathias, Grade Four, Woodridge Elementary, Alamo Heights ISD

A few weeks ago I went to my favorite place, Pet Works. I was just there to visit then the bunny got loose! I had to help the lady at the counter catch her, and the bunny's name is Lulu by the way. Here's the story.

It was just after school and my dad was dropping me off at Pet Works.

"Bye dad, see you at five o'clock!" I yelled.

I sprinted up the sidewalk and flung open the door. "Oh, my gosh." the place was a reck! "Hello?" Nobody was in site. Suddenly, Jamie, the counter lady, appered behind a huge stack of dog beds, carrying a net. "What's that big net for Jamie?" I curiously asked. "Lulu is loose somewhere in the store. Will you help me find her?" Jamie replied. "Of course I'll help, but I don't need a net." I said looking at Jamie with curious eyes.

So we started shearching around the store. I was looking behind some dog food when there Lulu sat. Before I could grab her or even call out Jamie's name she was off. She ran like lighting bouncing off the walls like a rubber or a bouncy ball. Jamie ran in the room after having no luck in the bird and fish room. She got one glance of Lulu and immediatly started to try and catch her in the net. She tried for 30 minutes but had no luck. Now it was my turn.

I grabbed the net from Jamie and started swinging like mad. Then….tharash!! I hit the net as hard as I could on the ground. It made Lulu stop running. It made the mice stop squeaking. It even made the birds stop squaking, screeching, crowing, and whistling. "Nows your chance Anna. Catch her." Jamie whispered in my ear. So I raised the net and lowered it in two seconds. I didn't catch her.

Lulu was ten or fifteen feet away now. So I ran and flung the net, and ran, I ran and flung a gillian times more. I was so tired out I could not walk! Then suddenly… Plop! She landed right in my arms.

"Jamie, Jamie, Jamie! I caught her! I caught Lulu!" "How?" she asked. "I just stood there and she hopped in my arms!" I replied back. "Wow." was all Jamie could say.

After we put Lulu in her cage and made sure it was locked, we heard Beep! Beep! "Oh, that's my dad Jamie. Gotta go! By!" I said and ran out the door.

I climbed in the car and as we drove off "I will always remember when I helped Jamie catch Lulu the bunny at Pet Works," I thought secretly to myself. And I never forgot.

Noah Alonzo, *A Time to Help: Little Hero*

Check our website
for reproducibles

Type of Minilesson: Dialogue Limitation

Writers combine dialogue with action.

Noah gracefully combines speech between two people with action all around both.

ACTIVITY:

Look at the fourth paragraph. Here's Noah's pattern:

1. Speech–speaker 1   2. Speech–speaker 2   3. Action
4. Speech–speaker 1   5. Action

CHALLENGE: Try inserting a pattern just like that into your own writing.

A Time to Help

Noah Alonzo, Grade Four, Murfee Elementary, Lubbock ISD

I have experienced a lot of things in my life. One by one, I see amazing things happen. I remember the most amazing thing that ever happened to me . . . I saved someone. It began late one night, when everyone was asleep. My mom drove around a corner, then my mom and I stared at a building on fire. "Uh oh," I thought.

My mom pulled over and got out of the car and told me to get out too. "Mom, what do you think happened?" I asked. "I don't know," she replied. "Heeeeelp!" someone inside the building yelled. "Mom, sorry I'm doing this, but I've got to save that person!" I stated. "Son, no!" she screamed, but I was already in the building.

The flames felt as hot as the sun, actually the flames felt hotter than the sun! "How am I going to find someone in here?" I asked myself. "Help! Help!" someone yelled. "Lucky me," I whispered. I sprinted to a closet guarded by flames. Luckily, I found a pail of water and put out the fire. Then I opened the door and spied a scared girl sitting in a corner of the closet.

"Sorry, but we have to go," I stated. "OK," she whispered. We ran faster than the speed of light. As we ran, I could hear the building coming down behind us. "Faster!" I yelled. Then we jumped out a window on the middle floor. For a moment, my heart stopped. Just when all hope was lost, two firemen saved us.

Beep, beep, beep went my heart on the scale. "Where am I?" I asked. "You're in the hospital," my mom answered. "Is she OK?" I asked. "Yes, she is, now get some rest, you need it you little hero," she replied.

Uriel Garcia, *Ironing*

Type of Minilesson: Layering Thinking

Writers let us inside their heads, telling us their thoughts as events happen.

Uriel uses remarkable inner speech, adding layers of thinking to his actions.

ACTIVITY:

Find a simple action sentence in your writing.

Ask yourself these questions, weaving the answers into your writing:

What was I wondering?

What did I think would happen?

What were the only things I knew right then?

For a second, what did I think?

Read Uriel's third paragraph to see where the questions come from.

CHALLENGE: Try using mental questions like these on your next piece.

Check our website
for reproducibles

Ironing

Uriel Garcia, Grade Seven, Herman Furlough Middle School, Terrell ISD

Dear Mom,

You have taught me to do a lot. For example: tie my shoes, how to use the bathroom, comb my hair, and a lot of other things. But one thing I will never forget, I want to thank you for. I think you can remember, I was 8 yrs. old and it was on a Sunday. It was tough but I got it. I still do it to this very day. It was a sunny Sunday, we were getting ready for church. Everybody was rushing. I was in my room looking for something clean to wear.

I had already taken a shower, all I needed was something to wear. You came in and told me to hurry up. So I decided to go under my bed and get some clothing from there. That was where all the dirty clothes were. But you didn't know. I grabbed some pants and a shirt and put them on. They smelled dirty and were all wrinkly. I was on my way out of the room, when all of a sudden I get pushed right back in. It was you of course.

I was wondering why! You told me to take all the clothes off. I did as you said. For some reason I knew we were going to be late. Everybody else was out of the house and gone. I thought we weren't going to church, but you did. You told me to go to your room, get the iron and the ironing board. I took it to my room and turned it on. I only knew three things about it. That it was very hot, and heavy. For a second there, I thought you were going to iron my clothes.

You told me to iron my clothes and all the rest of the clothes under the bed. At the time I was really confused. I've only seen you and Domingo use it. The other thing that I knew was that it gets your clothes very straight. I seen my brother use it a lot. You told me to stay here. I was at the house doing nothing but ironing. I got tired, but I just kept going and going. It was 2:30 in the afternoon when you got home. Everybody else was at my aunt's house.

You came in to my room smiling. I thought you were just being sarcastic. But you weren't. You told me I did okay. But that I could do better. I was ready to drop dead. So I just lay down on my bed. You were telling me that if I ever try to go to church with my pants not ironed, that you were going to spank me. So I never did. It always seems that if I'm not doing something else I will probably be ironing.

As you already know, I still do iron. I would probably say that no one in the family could iron more better than me. Not even you, and you taught me. I'm always telling you that I could do better at the cleaners than you. Not really though! But my ironing ways sure have changed a lot. Domingo tells me that I iron in the funniest way, but hey, it gets the job done.

Well anyways, I just wanted to thank you for teaching me how to do something I never thought I would end up doing. Last Saturday at Patty's party, I ironed Domingo's pants with starch, it came out so crazy. It even had me amazed. Well you sure have taught me a lot in my life. I just wanted to say thank you. Thank you for everything you do for us, as a mom and wife.

Love,

Uriel Garcia

Megan Weimorts, *Mittens*

Type of Minilesson: Blending Sentence Functions

Check our website
for reproducibles

To tell a story, writers use mixtures of speaking, thinking, viewing, and doing.

Megan skillfully blends these four kinds of writing in her piece, leaving readers perfectly clear about the whole memory.

ACTIVITY:

- This highlighting can be done by groups.

    Yellow: everything the narrator thought

    Blue: everything the narrator saw

    Pink: everything that anyone said

    Green: all the action (not counting thinking or talking)

    Share and compare what you notice.

CHALLENGE: Highlight something you've written in the same way, just to take a look at your own patterns.

Mittens

Megan Weimorts, Grade Four, Nolanville Elementary—Killeen ISD

As I walked up to my grandma's house, I saw my grandma. I thought to myself, "I wonder why she wants me to spend the night."

When I got up to the porch I waved bye to my mom and hugged my grandma. She said come in and set your bag down. I went in and did what she said. She offered me a glass of milk. Then she told me to follow her because she had something to show me. I put my milk down and did what she said. She opened a snowy white door and in there was so much sewing things I almost fell over. I was so shocked I could hardly say a word. She asked me if I wanted to help make mittens and I said yes. My grandma said we needed about six or seven pairs. We got the materials out and started working. She did one for example and showed me what it would look like when it's done. She brought in some band-aids just in case I accidentally poke myself with the needles. I grabbed the materials I needed and got to work. The first one didn't turn out too well, but I kept trying. After a little while I went to get a snack. When my grandma and I got in the kitchen I told my grandma that I already had three done. She said that I was pretty good for a six year old. Also she said that three was enough for today. That night when my grandma was asleep I crept into the sewing room to finish the mittens. When I was done with all the pairs of mittens I decided to make my grandma something. The next morning I gave my grandma a heart that had a picture of me on it. Above it said "I love you." Under the picture it said "By: Megan." My grandma said she liked it and then hung it up. After that we ate breakfast and then my grandma took me home. In the car she said thanks for helping.

I figured out that when my grandma let me help her I did something special for her because she let me.

RESEARCH ON FOUNDATIONS OF EFFECTIVE WRITING INSTRUCTION

"NCTE Beliefs about the Teaching of Writing," Writing Study Group of the National Council of Teachers of English (2004), ncte.org/positions/statements/writingbeliefs. [taken from the introduction of *Teaching the Neglected "R,"* Thomas Newkirk and Richard Kent Heinemann (2007), ncte.org/positions/statements/writingbeliefs.]

1. Everyone has the capacity to write, writing can be taught, and teachers can help students become better writers.
2. People learn to write by writing.
3. Writing is a process.
4. Writing is a tool for thinking.
5. Writing grows out of many different purposes.
6. Conventions of finished and edited texts are important to readers and therefore to writers.
7. Writing and reading are related.
8. Writing has a complex relationship to talk.
9. Literate practices are embedded in complicated social relationships.
10. Composing occurs in different modalities and technologies.
11. Assessment of writing involves complex, informed, human judgment.

"Guidelines for Teaching Middle and High School Students to Read and Write Well: Six Features of Effective Instruction," National Research Center on English Learning & Achievement, Dr. Judith A. Langer with Elizabeth Close, Janet Angelis, and Paula Preller, http://cela.albany.edu.

"Most classroom teachers work hard planning lessons, choosing materials, teaching classes, interacting with individual students, and assessing student progress. Yet some schools and teachers seem to be more successful than others. What makes the difference?" [p.2]

Six Features of Effective Instruction

1. Students learn skills and knowledge in multiple lesson types.
2. Teachers integrate test preparation into instruction.
3. Teachers make connections across instruction, curriculum, and life.
4. Students learn strategies for doing the work.
5. Students are expected to be generative thinkers.
6. Classrooms foster cognitive collaboration.

"It is important to understand that the six features identified in this research are interrelated and supportive of one another." [p.3]

A Report to Carnegie Corporation of New York, WRITING NEXT: Effective Strategies to Improve Writing of Adolescents in Middle Schools and High Schools, Steve Graham and Dolores Perin (2007), published by the Alliance for Excellent Education.

Recommendations: 11 Key Elements of Effective Adolescent Writing Instruction as Identified by Meta-Analysis

Effective Elements to Improve Writing Achievement in Grades Four to Twelve

1. Writing Strategies
2. Summarization
3. Collaborative Writing
4. Specific Product Goals
5. Word Processing
6. Sentence Combining
7. Prewriting
8. Inquiry Activities
9. Process Writing Approach
10. Study of Models
11. Writing for Content Learning

"The elements should not be seen as isolated but rather as interlinked . . . . A mixture of these elements is likely to generate the biggest return." [p.11]

Beliefs and Experiences

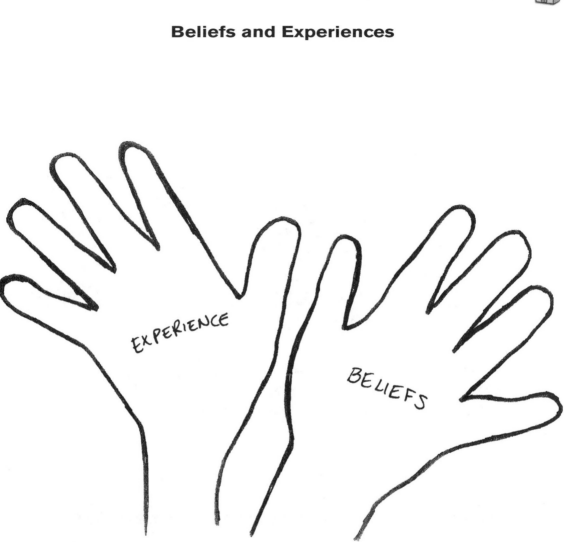

Beliefs and Experiences

Most really engaging pieces of writing have something from each hand.

Student Chart for Brainstorming "Bank Experiences"

Someone who made a difference in your life	Something important you lost	A time that someone hurt you, or you hurt someone	Something unexpected that happened	An important memory	A favorite memory	Something you'll never forget

■ STUDENT TOPIC LISTS

When asked to list things they could write a lot about, high school students suggested:

- the trauma of the emergency room
- the heartache of breaking up
- the fun of playing volleyball
- the heartbreak of losing someone
- the delay of the inevitable
- the joy of love
- the drama of friendship
- the instinct of survival
- the excitement of winning
- the fury of hatred
- the mystery of life
- the loneliness of being away
- the sadness of death
- the love of bubblegum
- the joy of writing
- the thrill of flying
- the confusion of life
- the horror of darkness
- the smell of an old book
- the excitement of new experiences
- the trauma of being lost
- the excitement of summer
- the sorrow of war
- the tragedy of time
- the shame of eating alone
- the stupidity of adults
- the fear of war in Iraq
- the melancholy of secrets
- flower pens
- bottle rockets
- Frisbees
- chocolate labs
- blue eyes
- license plates
- white t-shirts
- muddy tires
- braided bracelets
- ballpoint pens
- cowboy hats
- Superman
- planets
- red balloons
- diaries
- flip flops
- lollipops
- crocodiles
- hospital beds
- money
- paint ball
- guitar strings
- rocking chairs
- tortillas
- church
- waffles
- beaches
- monkeys
- golf clubs
- hairspray
- tractors
- confetti
- diamonds
- sunshine
- wax
- pie

■ STUDENT TOPIC LISTS *(continued)*

Fourth grade students suggested:

- horses
- monkeys
- dogs
- puppies
- flowers
- my own world
- my own horse
- fire
- vacations
- my teacher
- my friends
- my mom and dad
- my school
- someone special to me
- movies
- water
- my baby raccoon
- football
- basketball
- baseball
- the Army

- math
- NFL
- robots
- chickens
- United States
- national anthem
- money
- drawing
- history
- Indiana Jones
- school
- airplanes
- pizza
- my house
- ghosts
- a haunted house
- my cousin
- oceans
- lakes
- mountains

They also listed these "Stories I'd Like to Write":

- My Most Horrible Birthday (disasters)
- It Came from the Closet (scary)
- Frankenpizza (funny)
- A Diamond Robbery (mystery)
- A Fly's Life (nature)
- The Adventures of Bob (adventure)

■ QUICKLISTS FOR OTHER GENRES

Information Quicklist

3 things about the sky/planets/space you wish you knew:

1. How long will the sun burn?
2. Is there life out there?
3. Will we ever be space travelers?

3 things that are a danger to people:

1. Alcohol
2. Fast cars
3. Tornadoes

3 things that you wonder about bugs:

1. Do they have feelings?
2. Do they bond with their children?
3. Do they ever feel stressed out?

3 things that could make you sick:

1. Not wearing coats when it's cold
2. Being unfit
3. Not washing your hands

3 things that can make you healthier:

1. Exercise
2. Having friends
3. Eating right

3 things you know how to do:

3 things you know how to make:

3 things that have happened in your town in the past:

Persuasive Quicklist

3 customs/habits/rules at school you'd change:

1. Get rid of school uniforms
2. Make night school an option
3. Let students request teacher/parent conferences

3 customs/habits/rules in the community you'd change:

1. Enforce speed limits
2. Add sidewalks
3. Add a rec center in every neighborhood

3 customs/habits/rules in your country you'd change:

1. Build bullet trains between cities
2. Outlaw disposable food containers
3. Lower the voting age

3 customs/habits/rules in your world you'd change:

1. Get rid of light pollution
2. Get rid of war
3. End hunger

3 things you've bought in the last few months that gave you problems:

1. Crest toothpaste–tube is hard to squeeze
2. Black sweater–button came off
3. DVD–skipped the first time we played it

3 people who should get awards for something:

1. Giacomo Leone–most curious person
2. Johnny Ponce–most patient person
3. Dixie Shoopman–most wonderful mother

■ QUICKLISTS FOR OTHER GENRES *(continued)*

Literary Quicklist

A moment when a character changed:

1. The wolf's death

2. The first little pig's admiration for pig 3

A moment when a character tried to solve a problem:

1. When pig 3 took in pig 1 and pig 2

A moment when a character suffered:

1. Pig 2 during huffing and puffing

2. Wolf sliding into hot water

A moment when a character felt confused:

1. The moment the straw started to blow away

2. When the brick house didn't collapse

A moment when a character noticed a problem:

1. Pigs 1 and 2 when their houses started to collapse

2. When the wolf felt heat

A moment when a character tried to change something:

1. When pig 1 tried to talk pig 3 into building a faster house

2. When pig 3 tried to talk pig 1 into building a stronger house

Connecting Life Experiences to Life Truths

Students need time to reflect on their experiences to understand why the experiences stand out in their memories, what makes them important, and what they learned or how they changed as a result. The graphic organizer on page 148 gives students a way to sort through those experiences and understand their impact on themselves and others.

Connecting Life Experiences to Life Truths

LIFE TRUTHS ▼	LIFE EXPERIENCES ▶						
	Family	Friends	Unexpected or Unusual	Sports/ Hobbies	Problems/ Change	Injury/Death	Traditions
It was hard to learn							
I had to make a difficult choice							
I made a serious mistake							
I wish I hadn't done it							
Someone had a positive influence on my life							
I had a positive influence on someone's life							
Life taught me a lesson							
It was important for me to accept responsibility							
I didn't see it coming							
It was important to me to be open to new ideas							
Where I was (my surroundings) affected my life							
It was important for me to accept someone for who they are							
I'm responsible for finding my own "happy ending"							
A favorite person/ place/time							
One experience can have the power to affect my life in a positive way							

A MEMORY

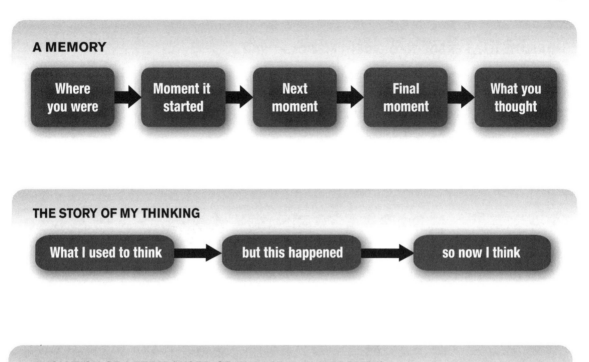

| Where you were | → | Moment it started | → | Next moment | → | Final moment | → | What you thought |

THE STORY OF MY THINKING

| What I used to think | → | but this happened | → | so now I think |

EVOLUTION OF A TERM (WORD OR PHRASE IN THE PROMPT)

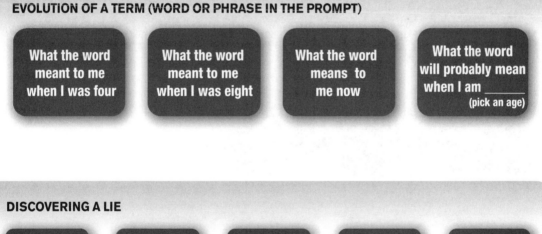

| What the word meant to me when I was four | What the word meant to me when I was eight | What the word means to me now | What the word will probably mean when I am _____ (pick an age) |

DISCOVERING A LIE

| Where you were | → | Moment it started | → | Next moment | → | Final moment | → | What you thought |

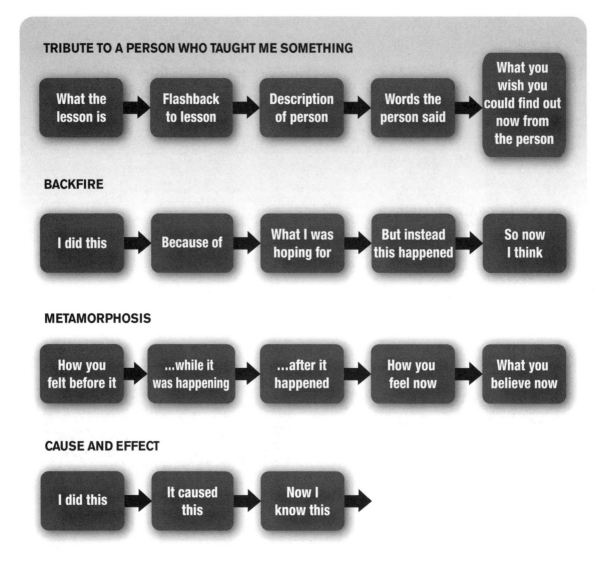

TRIBUTE TO A PERSON WHO TAUGHT ME SOMETHING

What the lesson is → Flashback to lesson → Description of person → Words the person said → What you wish you could find out now from the person

BACKFIRE

I did this → Because of → What I was hoping for → But instead this happened → So now I think

METAMORPHOSIS

How you felt before it → ...while it was happening → ...after it happened → How you feel now → What you believe now

CAUSE AND EFFECT

I did this → It caused this → Now I know this →

Expository, I-Search, and Literary Analysis Text Structures

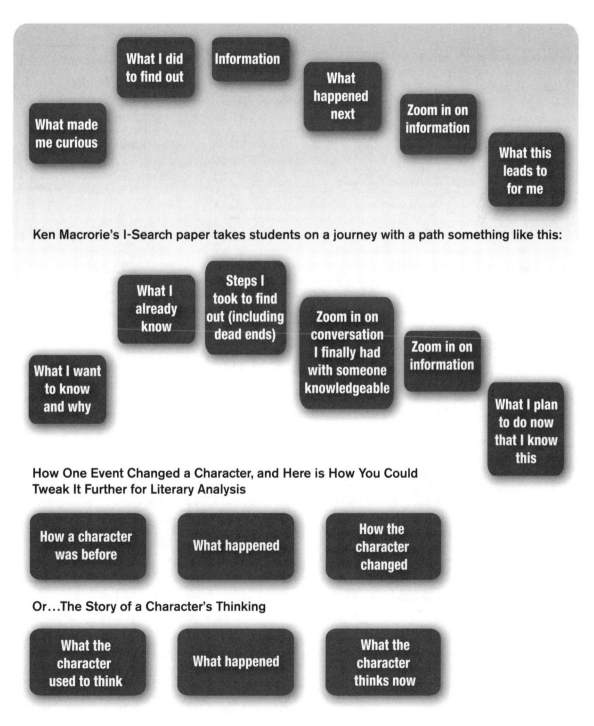

What I did to find out

Information

What happened next

Zoom in on information

What made me curious

What this leads to for me

Ken Macrorie's I-Search paper takes students on a journey with a path something like this:

What I already know

Steps I took to find out (including dead ends)

Zoom in on conversation I finally had with someone knowledgeable

Zoom in on information

What I want to know and why

What I plan to do now that I know this

How One Event Changed a Character, and Here is How You Could Tweak It Further for Literary Analysis

How a character was before

What happened

How the character changed

Or…The Story of a Character's Thinking

What the character used to think

What happened

What the character thinks now

Sample Pages of a Flipbook

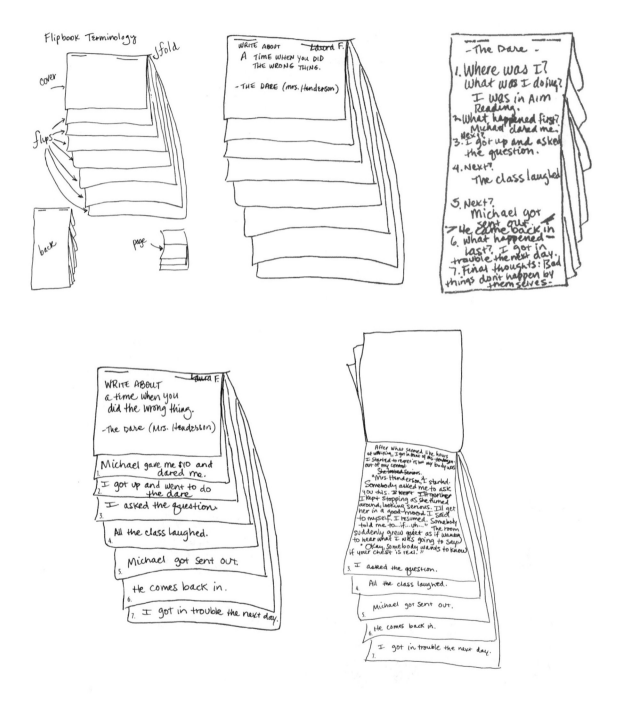

Revision Stations

REVISION STATION 1: SNAPSHOT CHALLENGE

1. Look at your sentence.
2. Imagine that you're looking at a photograph (or snapshot) taken at that moment.
3. Use words to describe everything you can see in the snapshot.

REVISION STATION 2: SENSES CHALLENGE

1. Look at your sentence.
2. Write details to show every one of the senses:
   - → What did you see?
   - → What did you hear?
   - → What did you smell?
   - → What did you feel?
   - → What did you taste?

REVISION STATION 3: THOUGHTSHOT CHALLENGE

1. Look at your sentence.
2. Imagine that people could hear everything you were thinking at that moment.
3. Write down everything that went through your head, everything you thought right then.

REVISION STATION 4: DIALOGUE CHALLENGE

1. Look at your sentence.
2. Imagine all of the conversation that went on at that moment.
3. Write down everything everyone said.

REVISION STATION 5: BA-DA-BING CHALLENGE

1. Look at your sentence.
2. Write one Ba-da-bing sentence for that moment, with these three parts:

Where your feet were right then   What your eye saw right then   What you thought right then

Cause and Effect (If . . . Then . . .)

CAUSE: You didn't use the flipbook correctly

IF... THEN...

You don't put the sequence of events with **actions,** *(not thoughts or feelings)* on your flips to organize your writing.	Your writing will become more and more vague and repetitive. You'll run out of anything to say.
You don't write "Where am I? What am I doing?" on the **first flip** so that when you begin writing, your FEET ARE ON THE GROUND inside the experience.	You don't know how to start, so your first paragraph is often vague and confusing. Then, you have a hard time getting started with writing the experience.
You don't set up your flipbook so that, page by page, you are *showing* what happened *next*—so that you can also show how you *reacted* to what happened next.	Your writing, by the third or fourth flip, will start to repeat. Since nothing new is happening, there's no new reaction . . . so you repeat what you've already said.
Before you started filling out the flipbook, you don't **figure out** and **write down** —on the FRONT COVER— what your **point** is for writing about *this* experience.	Your writing has no *focus,* no *undercurrent* of *purpose,* to guide it. After reading it, one could ask: **"Point? So what? Who's to care?"**
You convince yourself that the flipbook is a waste of your time. You set it up half-heartedly to please the teacher.	Your half-hearted flipbook leads to half-hearted writing that wanders confusingly from sentence to sentence.

EFFECT: Your writing becomes unfocused, confusing, vague, and repetitive.
In a word: boring.

Student Self-Check Flipbook

Self-Check: These Are the ABSOLUTE Requirements

Name_____Date_____

___1. I wrote the prompt down on the cover.

___2. I made a list of at least five experiences that show this.

___3. I wrote down what experience I chose to write about at the top of the back page.

___4. This planning lasted only fifteen to thirty minutes. No longer.

___5. I listed the things that happened (kernel essay) on the back of my flipbook.

___6. I moved that list to the flips on the front.

___7. I wrote *Where am I? What am I doing?* at the top of the first page . . . ONLY.

___8. I answered these two questions clearly before I wrote anything else on the first inside page.

___9. I am writing SIX OR MORE sentences on each inside page in TRIPLE SLOW MOTION, carefully connecting experience to the prompt.

Self-Check: These Are the ABSOLUTE Requirements

Name_____Date_____

___1. I wrote the prompt down on the cover.

___2. I made a list of at least five experiences that show this.

___3. I wrote down what experience I chose to write about at the top of the back page.

___4. This planning lasted only fifteen to thirty minutes. No longer.

___5. I listed the things that happened (kernel essay) on the back of my flipbook.

___6. I moved that list to the flips on the front.

___7. I wrote *Where am I? What am I doing?* at the top of the first page . . . ONLY.

___8. I answered these two questions clearly before I wrote anything else on the first inside page.

___9. I am writing SIX OR MORE sentences on each inside page in TRIPLE SLOW MOTION, carefully connecting experience to the prompt.

Self-Check: These Are the ABSOLUTE Requirements

Name_____Date_____

___1. I wrote the prompt down on the cover.

___2. I made a list of at least five experiences that show this.

___3. I wrote down what experience I chose to write about at the top of the back page.

___4. This planning lasted only fifteen to thirty minutes. No longer.

___5. I listed the things that happened (kernel essay) on the back of my flipbook.

___6. I moved that list to the flips on the front.

___7. I wrote *Where am I? What am I doing?* at the top of the first page . . . ONLY.

___8. I answered these two questions clearly before I wrote anything else on the first inside page.

___9. I am writing SIX OR MORE sentences on each inside page in TRIPLE SLOW MOTION, carefully connecting experience to the prompt.

Self-Check: These Are the ABSOLUTE Requirements

Name_____Date_____

___1. I wrote the prompt down on the cover.

___2. I made a list of at least five experiences that show this.

___3. I wrote down what experience I chose to write about at the top of the back page.

___4. This planning lasted only fifteen to thirty minutes. No longer.

___5. I listed the things that happened (kernel essay) on the back of my flipbook.

___6. I moved that list to the flips on the front.

___7. I wrote *Where am I? What am I doing?* at the top of the first page . . . ONLY.

___8. I answered these two questions clearly before I wrote anything else on the first inside page.

___9. I am writing SIX OR MORE sentences on each inside page in TRIPLE SLOW MOTION, carefully connecting experience to the prompt.

Student Self-Check Flipbook Final Copy

Self-Check: These Are the ABSOLUTE Requirements

Name_____Date_____

____ 1. I am writing my final copy in pencil.
____ 2. I started writing on the first line.
____ 3. I am indenting each time I start a new page on the flipbook.
____ 4. With dialogue, when I change speakers, I am changing paragraphs.
____ 5. I am using quotation marks with dialogue.
____ 6. I am capitalizing the first words of quotations.
____ 7. I am not skipping a blank line between paragraphs.
____ 8. My handwriting is small, neat, and easily readable.
____ 9. I am not gapping between words.
___10. I am not forgetting to space between all my words.
___11. I am putting periods at the end of all my sentences.
___12. I am capitalizing people's names.
___13. I am capitalizing the word "I."
___14. I am writing as neatly on the back as I did on the front.
___15. My truism RELATES TO *THE PROMPT.*

Self-Check: These Are the ABSOLUTE Requirements

Name_____Date_____

____ 1. I am writing my final copy in pencil.
____ 2. I started writing on the first line.
____ 3. I am indenting each time I start a new page on the flipbook.
____ 4. With dialogue, when I change speakers, I am changing paragraphs.
____ 5. I am using quotation marks with dialogue.
____ 6. I am capitalizing the first words of quotations.
____ 7. I am not skipping a blank line between paragraphs.
____ 8. My handwriting is small, neat, and easily readable.
____ 9. I am not gapping between words.
___10. I am not forgetting to space between all my words.
___11. I am putting periods at the end of all my sentences.
___12. I am capitalizing people's names.
___13. I am capitalizing the word "I."
___14. I am writing as neatly on the back as I did on the front.
___15. My truism RELATES TO *THE PROMPT.*

Self-Check: These Are the ABSOLUTE Requirements

Name_____Date_____

____ 1. I am writing my final copy in pencil.
____ 2. I started writing on the first line.
____ 3. I am indenting each time I start a new page on the flipbook.
____ 4. With dialogue, when I change speakers, I am changing paragraphs.
____ 5. I am using quotation marks with dialogue.
____ 6. I am capitalizing the first words of quotations.
____ 7. I am not skipping a blank line between paragraphs.
____ 8. My handwriting is small, neat, and easily readable.
____ 9. I am not gapping between words.
___10. I am not forgetting to space between all my words.
___11. I am putting periods at the end of all my sentences.
___12. I am capitalizing people's names.
___13. I am capitalizing the word "I."
___14. I am writing as neatly on the back as I did on the front.
___15. My truism RELATES TO *THE PROMPT.*

Self-Check: These Are the ABSOLUTE Requirements

Name_____Date_____

____ 1. I am writing my final copy in pencil.
____ 2. I started writing on the first line.
____ 3. I am indenting each time I start a new page on the flipbook.
____ 4. With dialogue, when I change speakers, I am changing paragraphs.
____ 5. I am using quotation marks with dialogue.
____ 6. I am capitalizing the first words of quotations.
____ 7. I am not skipping a blank line between paragraphs.
____ 8. My handwriting is small, neat, and easily readable.
____ 9. I am not gapping between words.
___10. I am not forgetting to space between all my words.
___11. I am putting periods at the end of all my sentences.
___12. I am capitalizing people's names.
___13. I am capitalizing the word "I."
___14. I am writing as neatly on the back as I did on the front.
___15. My truism RELATES TO *THE PROMPT.*

Scoring Guide

Score Point 1	Score Point 2	Score Point 3	Score Point 4
Because of the way you have written this, it is too hard to read and clearly understand. There are problems with punctuation, spelling, proper grammar, and so on. There is also a problem with you repeating the same thing too much. It's hard to tell that you read the prompt and are focused on what it says. I didn't get the feeling, as I read your paper, that you really cared whether you did a good job writing or not. Let's work on that.	I can usually follow and understand the experience you are writing about—although there are places where I got lost. There are too many problems with run-ons, capitalization, and spelling. There are also problems with repeating and with this sounding more like a list of what happened instead of an explanation and showing of it. I often needed to reread and try to figure out what you had written . . . or what you had probably meant to write.	Your paper was basically clear from beginning to end. While there were some problems with correct punctuation and spelling, these did not keep me from being able to easily read and understand what you wrote. You shared your reactions and thoughts consistently. Some observations were uniquely exceptional. Your ending was clear and appropriate to your focus. If you had proofread (more) carefully, most of the errors could have been corrected.	Your writing captured me from the beginning. Where you were, I was. What you saw, I saw. What you thought and felt, I could understand and identify with. Your language skills added both clarity and meaning to your writing. My first thought when I finished reading your paper was, "Wow! I hope I can have a copy of this!" Thank you for taking the time and effort to produce writing of this quality.

Score Point 1	Score Point 2	Score Point 3	Score Point 4
Because of the way you have written this, it is too hard to read and clearly understand. There are problems with punctuation, spelling, proper grammar, and so on. There is also a problem with you repeating the same thing too much. It's hard to tell that you read the prompt and are focused on what it says. I didn't get the feeling, as I read your paper, that you really cared whether you did a good job writing or not. Let's work on that.	I can usually follow and understand the experience you are writing about—although there are places where I got lost. There are too many problems with run-ons, capitalization, and spelling. There are also problems with repeating and with this sounding more like a list of what happened instead of an explanation and showing of it. I often needed to reread and try to figure out what you had written . . . or what you had probably meant to write.	Your paper was basically clear from beginning to end. While there were some problems with correct punctuation and spelling, these did not keep me from being able to easily read and understand what you wrote. You shared your reactions and thoughts consistently. Some observations were uniquely exceptional. Your ending was clear and appropriate to your focus. If you had proofread (more) carefully, most of the errors could have been corrected.	Your writing captured me from the beginning. Where you were, I was. What you saw, I saw. What you thought and felt, I could understand and identify with. Your language skills added both clarity and meaning to your writing. My first thought when I finished reading your paper was, "Wow! I hope I can have a copy of this!" Thank you for taking the time and effort to produce writing of this quality.

The Fake Flipbook

Cover	Flip 2 What happened first?
Flip 1 Where was I? What was I doing?	Flip 3 What happened next?

The Fake Flipbook (continued)

Flip 4 What happened next?

Flip 6 What happened next?

Flip 5 What happened next?

Flip 7 What was the last thing that happened? Final
thoughts?

Where's the BEEF?

Elaboration–Where's the BEEF!!!!!!!!!!!!?
(Brain, Ear, Eyes, Feet)

What would your brain be thinking?

What would you be hearing?

What would you see?

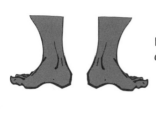

What are your feet doing?

Elaboration–Where's the BEEF!!!!!!!!!!!!?
(Brain, Ear, Eyes, Feet)

Describe what your brain was thinking.

Describe what you would be hearing.

Describe what you would see.

Describe what your feet are doing.

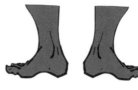

Have students place a copy of this handout in their writing journal and in their homework folder for a quick revising guide.

F.I.T. Chart

Topic _____

Prompt _____

Truism (Life Lesson) _____

F.eelings	I.nformation	T.houghts (or speaking)

KISS Lesson Plan

WEEK 1		
Monday	Make class WRITER'S TOOLBOX chart	30 minutes
	Introductory TRUISMS lesson	30 minutes
Tuesday	Minilesson "The Bunny Escape" on sensory words	15 minutes
	Write a KERNEL ESSAY	45 minutes
Wednesday	Discuss more photos and truisms	10 minutes
	Write compositions	50 minutes
Thursday	GREAT BEGINNINGS, SPARKLING SENTENCES	15 minutes
	Write final copy, share with partner	45 minutes

WEEK 2		
Monday	Share and discuss TRUISMS	10 minutes
	Make QUICKLIST, fill out "A Memory" TEXT STRUCTURE	50 minutes
Tuesday	Minilesson "A Time to Help" on dialogue	15 minutes
	Write a rough draft of essay, skipping lines for revising	45 minutes
Wednesday	Introduce and share BA-DA-BING SENTENCES	15 minutes
	Write compositions, revising to add Ba-da-bing Sentences	45 minutes
Thursday	Read aloud two or three essays, compare Quicklists to common prompts	15 minutes
	Write, edit, and proofread final copy	45 minutes

WEEK 3		
Monday	Write a KERNEL ESSAY	20 minutes
	Transfer Kernel Essay to FLIPBOOK	40 minutes
Tuesday	Minilesson on "Ironing" on layering thinking	15 minutes
	Expand flipbook by writing inside pages	45 minutes
Wednesday	Minilesson on using REVISION STATIONS	20 minutes
	Rotate through Revision Stations	40 minutes
Thursday	Read aloud samples, post Sparkling Sentences	10 minutes
	Write final copy	50 minutes

WEEK 4		
Monday	Minilesson "Mittens" on blending sentence functions	20 minutes
	Write Kernel Essay, use "The Story of My Thinking" structure	40 minutes
Tuesday	Share and discuss TRUISMS	10 minutes
	Minilesson on Common Mistakes, finish rough draft	50 minutes
Wednesday	Model using Let's Get F.I.T. chart	15 minutes
	Copy rough draft onto F.I.T. chart	45 minutes
Thursday	Minilessons The Final Copy	10 minutes
	Write final copy, proofread	50 minutes
Friday	CELEBRATION!	60 minutes

Writer's Toolbox

Similes

...a hotel that looked like a palace in one of those royalty movies. (Desiree M.)

Bada-bings

When I stepped into the classroom and noticed that Angela's desk was empty, I wondered what happened. (Raymond C.)

Dialogue

"What's that big net for, Jamie?" I curiously asked.

"Lulu is loose somewhere in the store." (Anna M.)

Sparkling Sentences

It's hard because I think one thing and then another. (Julio T.) and

Haha, get that nine to five, baby bro. (Carlos T.)

Truisms

You don't always have to have the best to make you feel whole inside. (Dustin H.)

Minilessons

Anna Matthias, *The Bunny Escape,* p. 130

Type of Minilesson: Sensory Words

Writers don't use every strategy they know all the time. They pick and choose whatever works best for each situation.

Anna treats her readers to a masterful flurry of noise, not from beginning to end, but just when the story truly gets noisy.

ACTIVITY:
- Read the piece.
- Highlight the words and phrases that bring sounds to a reader's imaginary ear. Notice where those words and phrases are concentrated.

Examples: thrash, squeaking, squawking, screeching, crowing, whistling, whispered.

CHALLENGE: Find (or build) a moment in your own writing where there's a sensory flurry. Add enough sensory words so that a reader's imaginary senses feel it.

Noah Alonzo, *A Time to Help: Little Hero,* p. 132

Type of Minilesson: Dialogue Limitation

Writers combine dialogue with action.

Noah gracefully combines speech between two people with action all around both.

ACTIVITY:

Look at the fourth paragraph. Here's Noah's pattern:

> Speech–speaker 1
>
> Speech–speaker 2
>
> Action
> Speech–speaker 1
>
> Action

CHALLENGE: Try inserting a pattern just like that into your own writing.

Minilessons

Uriel Garcia, *Ironing,* p. 133

Type of Minilesson: Layering Thinking

Writers let us inside their heads, telling us their thoughts as events happen.

Uriel uses remarkable inner speech, adding layers of thinking to his actions.

ACTIVITY:

Find a simple action sentence in your writing.

Ask yourself these questions, weaving the answers into your writing:

What was I wondering?

What did I think would happen?

What were the only things I knew right then?

For a second, what did I think?

Read Uriel's third paragraph to see where the questions come from.

CHALLENGE: Try using mental questions like these on your next piece.

Megan Weimorts, *Mittens,* p. 135

Type of Minilesson: Blending Sentence Functions

To tell a story, writers use mixtures of speaking, thinking, viewing, and doing.

Megan skillfully blends these four kinds of writing in her piece, leaving readers perfectly clear about the whole memory.

ACTIVITY:

- This highlighting can be done by groups.

    Yellow: everything the narrator thought

    Blue: everything the narrator saw

    Pink: everything that anyone said

    Green: all the action (not counting thinking or talking)

    Share and compare what you notice.

CHALLENGE: Highlight something you've written in the same way, just to take a look at your own patterns.

WORKS CITED

Bernabei, Gretchen. 2001. *Lightning In a Bottle*. San Antonio, TX: Trail of Breadcrumbs.

Bernabei, Gretchen. 2005. *Reviving the Essay: How to Teach Structure without Formula*. Shoreham, VT: Discover Writing Press.

Bernabei, Gretchen and Judi Reimer, ed. 2008. *Sparklers: High Scoring Test Essays and What We Learn From Them*. San Antonio: Trail of Breadcrumbs.

Brock, Paula. 2002. *Nudges: Thinking, Writing, Vocabulary, and Spelling*. Spring, TX: Absey and Co.

Campbell, Walter Stanley. 1950. *Writing: Advice and Devices*. New York: Doubleday.

Culham, Ruth. 2003. *6+1 Traits of Writing*. New York: Scholastic, NREL.

Graham, S. and Perin, D. 2007. *Writing Next*. New York: Carnegie Corporation.

Lane, Barry. 1993. *After the End: Teaching and Learning Creative Revision*. Portsmouth, NH: Heinemann.

Langer, Judith. 2000. *Guidelines for Teaching Middle and High School Students to Read and Write Well: Six Features of Effective Instruction*. Albany: National Research Center on English Learning and Achievement.

Macrorie, Ken. 1988. *The I-Search Paper: Revised Edition of Searching Writing*. Portsmouth, NH: Boynton-Cook.

McKee, Paul and M. Lucile Harrison. 1947. *Let's Talk: Language for Meaning*. Boston: Houghton Mifflin.

Nasar, Sylvia, ed. 2008. *The Best American Science Writing*. New York: Harper Perennial.

Newkirk, Thomas. 1989. *The Critical Thinking and Writing Series: Reclaiming the Essay*. NCTE/ERIC. Reprinted as *The School Essay Manifesto*. 2005. Shoreham, VT: Discover Writing Press.

Newkirk, Thomas and Richard Kent, ed. 2007. *Teaching the Neglected R: Rethinking Writing Instruction in Secondary Classrooms.* Portsmouth, NH: Heinemann.

Zike, Dinah. 2008. *Notebook Foldables for Binders, Spirals, and Composition Books.* San Antonio, TX: Dinah-Might Adventures.

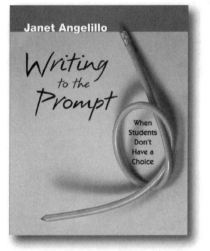

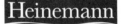